Angels Walk Among Us

Don Litton

Halo
PUBLISHING
INTERNATIONAL

Copyright © 2019 Don Litton
All rights reserved.

No part of this book may be reproduced in any manner without the written consent of the publisher except for brief excerpts in critical reviews or articles.

ISBN: 978-1-61244-758-2
Library of Congress Control Number: 2019908041

Printed in the United States of America

Halo Publishing International
1100 NW Loop 410
Suite 700 - 176
San Antonio, Texas 78213
www.halopublishing.com
contact@halopublishing.com

Acknowledgment

Writing a book was harder than I thought and more rewarding than I could have ever imagined. No one in life does anything worthwhile alone. So, in my case I have several special people to acknowledge. My wife, Janice, has kept me, comforted and has for years put up with my crazy schedule, mainly my daytime and nighttime hours being in reverse order. Her love for Christ and me has allowed me great freedom to execute my calling. The members of Friendship Baptist Church in Fishville, La "endured my preaching and teaching" for 13 years, until January of 2018. They were a captive audience for my stories and not so humorous jokes; they would even groan when I began to tell them.

I would not have made it this far in my book had not my sister, Rita Litton Ellis, spent countless hours reading, correcting, and revising sentences and paragraphs of my manuscript. More importantly, I thank God for the journey, age 73, and to have KNOWN HIM for 58 years. Being a reborn Christian, the Lord has guided me with HIS eye and it has been an insane walk with HIM. Only a foolish man would say I know a lot about God because in my case the more I have learned about HIM, the less I realized I know.

Contents

Foreword   9

Introduction   13

Chapter 1   15
Origin of Angels

Chapter 2   31
Angelic Organization

Chapter 3   53
Mission of Angels

Chapter 4   75
Names of Angels

Chapter 5   101
Fallen Angels or Demons

Chapter 6   117
Encounters with Angels

Chapter 7   133
Gathering of the Angels

References	153
Appendix	157
Angels – 100 Verses	157
Photos of Angels by Don Litton	173

Foreword

For over 30 years I have contended for miracles and the tangible manifestation of the Holy Spirit. This quest has actually taken me to 5 continents and too many worship experiences and in diverse languages and cultures to list here. In this journey my heart has been to experience the power of our risen Christ for myself and to hear the glorious testimonies of those who have been dramatically transformed by this living Savior . We have witnessed those who have been raised from the dead, the blind receive sight, cripples who now walking and the deaf that now hear.

It was on this journey of tracking testimonies and celebrating the goodness of our God that I first heard of the ministry of Dr. Don Litton. I received a call years ago from a missionary friend in Brazil who was ecstatic over the incredible revival of miracles and deliverance he was experiencing in Brazil. He began to share testimonies of incredible documented miracles of healing that had me on the edge of my seat. He actually shared he had seen more instant healings and deliverance in 1 week than he had seen in his ministry. One story that made my heart rejoice was to hear that even the deaf and crippled beggars that he knew from seeing on the streets as beggars were healed in these meetings. So, of course, I asked who this guest minister was who was seeing such a manifestation of the Kingdom. That's the first time I heard the name of Don

Litton, and it was a moment that changed our lives. Living in Louisiana at the time I couldn't believe that the man walking in this level of faith and the miraculous was a Southern Baptist pastor who lived only a couple of hours away.

From the very first moment I called Dr. Litton on the phone there was a Divine connection. As he began to tell me his journey in ministry and secular education I was amazed at the incredible stories and testimonies that he shared. This began a friendship that has continued over 10 years! Beginning just a few weeks from that first phone connection I invited him to minister at our Church. It was absolutely incredible! The very first meeting over 50 people testified to instant physical miracles of healing. We saw deaf ears open, cripples walked and people I had watched suffer for years healed instantly by the power of God. Over the next few months we would hear testimonies of at least 200 people who had been healed or set free from spiritual bondage through this ministry.

The simplicity of the Gospel presented from someone with such a background from academia as an educator was astounding and refreshing at the same time. It was so enlightening for us to hear Pastor Litton's perspective on the gifts of the Spirit and the supernatural evidence of the work of the Holy Spirit. This began a friendship where for years Doc has ministered and encouraged our entire family. There have been days he would just show up to my office and folk would hear and begin to gather at the Church and the miracles would begin.

It was after these times of ministry and fellowship that he would enthrall us with his encounters with angels. Not only did he have personal stories, but so many other testimonies of others who had witnessed as well. It was always so interesting to me because for those who have discounted such experiences as only for the desperate, illiterate or ignorant, that such teaching and testimony come from one so esteemed and educated in the secular. I loved hearing such simple faith from one who although learned in so many areas, had learned to truly apply the Gospel of the Kingdom. To have the wisdom and knowledge of a ministry that spans over 50 years while at the same time maintaining child-like faith is extraordinary and extremely valuable we the reader as we peruse the pages of these incredible encounters.

In these pages you will have the opportunity to meet my friend, to hear these incredible testimonies of Heaven touching earth. True testimonies even with documented photographs and eye witness accounts will keep you riveted to the pages of this book. You will have the opportunity for your faith to arise to another level and the word of God come alive as you believe you can have your own personal miraculous moment.

I can't wait for you to experience the heart of my friend in this work and be as blessed as I have been by knowing him.

In Christ Alone,
Jonathan Suber
Senior Pastor
Oasis Church
Austin, Texas

Introduction

At this very moment, there is a vast supernatural reality all around you. You can not see it, but this other realm encompasses angelic beings and spiritual powers. Who are these mysterious creatures that adorn decorations and stir imaginations? What do angels do, and what is their purpose? Does the Bible have anything to say about this different reality? Yes, it does! The mention of angels is inclusive in scripture. In the NASB translation, these celestial beings are referred to 196 times, 103 times in the Old Testament and 93 times in the New Testament. These references are scattered throughout the Bible and are found in at least 34 books, from the first book Genesis to the last book of the Bible Revelation (Ryrie, 1987).

Angels are spiritual beings created by God to serve Him, though created higher than man. Some, the good angels, have remained obedient to Him and carry out His will, while others, fallen angels, disobeyed, fell from their holy position, and now stand in active opposition to the work and plan of God. Due to the inspired and inerrant character of Scripture, we can trust completely in the Bible's teaching on angels. Paul wrote:

> **Colossians 1:16** - "For by Him all things were created, both in the heavens and on earth, visible and invisible, whether thrones or dominions or rulers or authorities (a reference to angels) all things have been created by Him and for Him" **(KJV)**.

The study of angels or the doctrine of angelology is one of the ten major categories of theology developed in many systematic theological works. However, in the world of religions, there seems to be a somewhat distorted view of what the Bible teaches about the subject of angels. It is out of an extended body of Scripture that the doctrine of angels, as presented here, will be developed. The objective of this writing is to make the Bible our authority on the subject of angels rather than man's experiences, speculations, and what may or may not sound logical.

Chapter 1
Origin of Angels

The English word angel is derived from the Greek word angelos, which means "messenger." Christians and others from the world's major religions believe that angels are messengers from God who carry out tasks that God assigns to them on behalf of humans on earth. Angels are powerful spiritual beings who serve God and human beings in a wide variety of ways (Evans, 1912).

Christianity and Judaism all say that an essential part of the work of angels is simply worshiping the God who created them, such as by praising Him in heaven. Religions, such as Christianity, say that some angels are faithful to God while others have rebelled against him and are now known as demons. Other religions, such as Islam, say that all angels serve God faithfully.

Angels may appear on earth in either human form or heavenly form. They may be disguised to look just like human beings or may appear as often depicted in popular art with human faces and mighty wings, often shining with light from within. Angels don't just stand around in heaven; they have lots of work to do because they are ministering spirits:

Hebrews 1:14 - "Are they not all ministering spirits, sent forth to minister for them who shall be heirs of salvation" (**KJV**)?

The exact time of the creation of angels is never stated in the Bible, but we know they were created before the world was created. The book of Job tells us they were present when the earth was created:

> **Job 38:4-7** - "Where wast thou when I laid the foundations of the earth? declare, if thou hast understanding. Who hath laid the measures thereof, if thou knowest? or who hath stretched the line upon it? Whereupon are the foundations thereof fastened? or who laid the corner stone thereof; When the morning stars sang together, and all the sons of God shouted for joy" **(KJV)**?

So we see their origin was before the creation of the earth which is described in the first chapter of Genesis. Angels are created beings and not the spirits of departed or glorified human beings as brought out in **Psalm 148**. The Psalmist calls on all in the celestial heavens, including the angels, to praise God for a reason:

> **Psalm 148:1-5** - "Praise ye the LORD. Praise ye the LORD from the heavens: Praise him in the heights. Praise ye him, all his angels: praise ye him, all his hosts. Praise ye him, sun and moon: praise him, all ye stars of light. Praise him, ye heavens of heavens, and ye waters that be above the heavens. Let them praise the name of the LORD: for he commanded, and they were created" **(KJV)**.

The great hosts of angels and everything in the celestial heavens are proclaimed to be created by God and directed to praise the name of the Lord.

God created man and the animal kingdom in pairs with the ability and the responsibility to procreate. Angels, however, were created simultaneously as a host or a company.

Colossians 1:16 - "For by him were all things created, that are in heaven, and that are in earth, visible and invisible, whether they be thrones, or dominions, or principalities, or powers: all things were created by him, and for him" **(KJV)**.

Nehemiah 9:6 - "Thou, even thou, art LORD alone; thou hast made heaven, the heaven of heavens, with all their host, the earth, and all things that are therein, the seas, and all that is therein, and thou preservest them all; and the host of heaven worshippeth thee" **(KJV)**.

Angels do not propagate or multiply themselves as with humans. There is never any mention in the bible of the death of angels.

Luke 20:36 - "Neither can they die any more: for they are equal unto the angels; and are the children of god, being the children of the resurrection" **(KJV)**.

Hebrews 9:27 says, "And as it is appointed unto men once to die, but after this the judgment" **(KJV)**.

Angels who have fallen from grace will be judged in the future and permanently confined to the lake of fire ordained by angels in the hand of a mediator. The writer to the Hebrews says:

Hebrews 2:2 - "For if the word spoken by angels was stedfast, and every transgression and disobedience received a just recompence of reward" **(KJV)**.

References:

Matthew 25:41 - "Then shall he say also unto them on the left hand, Depart from me, ye cursed, into everlasting fire, prepared for the devil and his angels" **(KJV)**.

II Peter 2:4 - "For if God spared not the angels that sinned, but cast them down to hell, and delivered them into chains of darkness, to be reserved unto judgment" **(KJV)**.

Jude 6 - "And the angels which kept not their first estate, but left their own habitation, he hath reserved in everlasting chains under darkness unto the judgment of the great day" **(KJV)**.

Nevertheless, they are an innumerable host created by God before the creation of the earth.

References:

Nehemiah 9:6 - "Thou, even thou, art LORD alone; thou hast made heaven, the heaven of heavens, with all their host, the earth, and all things that are therein, the seas, and all that is therein, and thou preservest them all; and the host of heaven worshippeth thee" **(KJV)**.

Hebrews 12:22 - "But ye are come unto mount Sion, and unto the city of the living God, the heavenly Jerusalem, and to an innumerable company of angels" **(KJV)**.

Daniel 7:10 - "A fiery stream issued and came forth from before him: thousand thousands ministered unto him, and ten thousand times ten thousand stood before him: the judgment was set, and the books were opened" **(KJV)**.

Matthew 26:53 - "Thinkest thou that I cannot now pray to my Father, and he shall presently give me more than twelve legions of angels" **(KJV)**?

Revelation 5:11 - "And I beheld, and I heard the voice of many angels round about the throne, and the beasts and the elders: and the number of them was ten thousand times ten thousand, and thousands of thousands" **(KJV)**.

Matthew 22:28-30 - "Therefore in the resurrection whose wife shall she be of the seven? for they all had her. Jesus answered and said unto them, Ye do err, not knowing the scriptures, nor the power of God. For in the resurrection they neither marry, nor are given in marriage, but are as the angels of God in heaven" **(KJV)**.

Psalm 104:2-6 - "You stretched out the heavens like a tent, You set the beams of your chambers on the waters, You make the clouds your chariot, You ride on the wings of the wind You make the winds your angels, Fire and flame your ministers. You set the earth on its foundations. So that it shall never be shaken. You cover it with the deep as with a garment; The waters stood above the mountains" **(NIV)**.

In this account of creation we read "you make the winds your angels," and early interpreters took this as an indication that God created angels in the beginning. It was now up to them to discover how it fits into the story of creation in Genesis (Ryrie, 1987).

Genesis 1:1 says: "In the beginning, God created the heaven and the earth" **(KJV)**.

The plan to create the heavens and earth was announced and subsequently completed. Ancient interpreters found one way of connecting the creation of angels to Genesis by what:

Genesis 2:1 says: "Thus the heavens and the earth were finished, and all the host of them" **(KJV)**.

This verse adds the word "host." What does that mean and how is it interpreted?

Some early interpreters took this to mean that angels were created sometime during the six days of creation in **Genesis 1**, even though they weren't mentioned there explicitly. It seems clear from the context that "host" refers to whatever God had made to occupy the heavens and the earth. Hence, the **NIV** version says "and all their vast array," and the **NRSV** version says "and all their multitude." Other versions of the written word of God seems to refer specifically to the stars:

> **Daniel 8:10** - "It grew until it reached the host of the heavens, and it threw some of the starry host down to the earth and trampled on them" **(NIV)**.

> **Zephaniah 1:5** - "Those who bow down on the roofs to the host of the heavens; those who bow down and swear to the LORD, but also swear by Milcom;" **(NRSV)**.

It can also refer to an angelic group of some sort. For example:

> **I Kings 22:19** reads: "Then Micaiah said, 'Therefore hear the word of the Lord: I saw the Lord sitting on his throne, with all the host of heaven standing beside him to the right and to the left of him'" **(NIV)**.

Again in **Psalm 148:2**, we read: "Praise him, all his angels; praise him, all his hosts" **(KJV)**.

Early interpreters do not all agree on precisely where in the six-day sequence to place the creation of angels. Even though **Genesis 1** does not mention the creation of angels, a number of interpreters included them among God's works in the six days. It seemed logical that they were created before humans. Angels came first, before any other created thing. **Genesis 1** is not explicit about the creation of angels, but it is possible that they are alluded to in the "heavens" in **verse 1** or the "light" in **verse 3**. The solutions differ, but all are trying to address the problem of where in **Genesis 1** the creation of angels is mentioned.

Still, other interpreters found the creation of angels on day two when the firmament was created. Since angels reside above somewhere, they may have been created along with the firmament. Some say that **Genesis 1:20**, places the creation of angels on day five **(KJV)**. Why? That is when God created winged birds, and in **Isaiah 6**, we read of angels with two wings who fly about:

> **Isaiah 6:2** - "Above it stood the seraphims: each one had six wings; with twain, he covered his face, and with twain, he covered his feet, and with twain, he did fly" **(KJV)**.

Some readers may say that God was not overly concerned with the creation of angels in **Genesis** and leave it at that. I think that is the correct answer, but such an answer did not satisfy early interpreters, especially given what they read in **Psalm 104**. Even though Genesis is silent, there were enough clues elsewhere in the written word to invite ancient interpreters to read more deeply.

Old Testament

- *Present at Creation*

> **Job 38:4-7** - "Where were you when I laid the earth's foundation? Tell me, if you understand. Who marked off its dimensions? Surely you know! Who stretched a measuring line across it? On what were its footings set, or who laid its cornerstone, while the morning stars sang together and all the angels shouted for joy" **(KJV)**?

- *Hagar*

Although angels were most likely present at creation, there is no mention of their ministry until the days of Abraham. After Hagar had conceived Abraham's child, she was sent away by Sarah, Abraham's wife. The angel of the LORD found Hagar:

> **Genesis 16:7** - "The angel of the LORD found her by a spring of water in the wilderness, the spring on the way to Shur" **(KJV)**.

Later, when Hagar and Ishmael were sent out by Abraham and Sarah, the Bible says that an angel ministered unto them.

> **Genesis 21:17** - "And God heard the voice of the lad; and the angel of God called to Hagar out of heaven, and said unto her, What aileth thee, Hagar? fear not; for God hath heard the voice of the lad where he is" **(KJV)**.

- *Three angels visit Abraham*

The Bible says that three angels visited Abraham while on their way to Sodom. These angels appeared in the form of men.

> **Genesis 18:2** - "He looked up and saw three men standing nearby. When he saw them, he ran from the tent entrance to meet them and bowed down to the ground" **(RSV)**.

The "Angel of the LORD" was one of the angels who met Abraham.

- *Jacob*

Jacob had a variety of experiences with angels. One of these episodes was his famous dream. He had a dream in which:

Genesis 28:12 - "He dreamed that there was a ladder set up on the earth, the top of it reaching to heaven; and the angels of God were ascending and descending on it. He saw a stairway resting on the earth, with its top reaching to heaven, and the angels of God were ascending and descending on it" **(RSV)**.

An angel appeared to Jacob in another dream:

Genesis 31:11 - "Then the angel of God said to me in the dream, Jacob, and I said, 'Here am I'" **(KJV)**.

Later, angels met Jacob as he traveled.

Genesis 32:1 - "Jacob went on his way, and the angels of God met him" **(KJV)**.

At the end of his life, Jacob said:

Genesis 48:16 - "The Angel which redeemed me from all evil, bless the lads; and let my name be named on them, and the name of my fathers Abraham and Isaac; and let them grow into a multitude in the midst of the earth" **(KJV)**.

Jacob had many experiences with angels throughout his life.

- *Passover Angel*

The angel of death killed every firstborn, of both humans and animals, of those families who did not have blood placed over the door post. The families of those who placed the blood were passed over by the angel of death as told in **Exodus 12**.

- *Giving of the Law*

Angels were present at the giving of the law:

Deuteronomy 33:2 - "And he said, The LORD came from Sinai, and rose up from Seir unto them; he shined forth from mount Paran, and He came with ten thousands of saints: from his right hand went a fiery law for them" **(KJV)**.

Psalm 68:17 - "The chariots of God are twenty thousand, even thousands of angels: the Lord is among them, as in Sinai, in the holy place" **(KJV)**.

- *Warning to Balaam*

When God sent His angel to warn Balaam that he was disobeying the Lord, Balaam's donkey said to him:

Numbers 22:30-31 - "Am I not your donkey, which you have ridden all your life to this day? Have I been in the habit of treating you this way?" And he said, 'No.' Then the LORD opened the eyes of Balaam, and he saw the angel of the LORD standing in the road, with his drawn sword in his hand; and he bowed down, falling on his face" **(KJV)**.

- *Rebuke of Israel*

An angel rebuked Israel for their idolatry:

Judges 2:1-4 - "And an angel of the LORD came up from Gilgal to Bochim, and said, I made you to go up out of Egypt, and have brought you unto the land which I sware unto your fathers; and I said, I will never break my covenant with you. And ye shall make no league with the inhabitants of this land; ye shall throw down their altars: but ye have not obeyed my voice: why have ye done this? Wherefore I also said, I will not drive them out from before you, but they shall be as thorns in your sides, and their gods shall be a snare unto you. And it came to pass, when the angel of the LORD spake these words unto all the children of Israel, that the people lifted up their voice, and wept" **(KJV)**.

- ***Curse Enemies Of The Lord***

During the time of the Judges, an angel cursed those who did not help the LORD against His enemies:

Judges 5:23 - "Curse Meroz, says the angel of the LORD, curse bitterly its inhabitants because they did not come to the help of the LORD, to the help of the LORD against the mighty" **(KJV)**.

- ***Judged Israel for David's Sin***

When David sinned by numbering the people of Israel, God judged them through the angel of the LORD. However, when the angel stretched out his hand toward Jerusalem to destroy it, the LORD relented concerning the evil, and said to the angel who was bringing destruction among the people:

II Samuel 24:1-17 - "It is enough; now stay your hand. The angel of the LORD was then by the threshing floor of Araunah the Jebusite. When David saw the angel who was destroying the people, he said to the LORD, I alone have sinned, and I alone have done wickedly; but these sheep, what have they done? Let your hand, I pray, be against me and against my father's house" **(KJV)**.

- ***Elijah Strengthened By Angel***

The prophet Elijah was strengthened by an angel who brought him food to eat and water to drink along his journey:

I Kings 19:5-7 - "Then he laid down under the broom tree and fell asleep. Suddenly an angel touched him and said to him, 'Get up and eat.' He looked, and there at his head was a cake baked on hot stones and a jar of water. He ate and drank and laid down again. The angel of the LORD came a second time, touched him, and said, 'Get up and eat'; otherwise the journey will be too much for you'" **(NLT)**.

- *Angel Killed the Assyrians*

The angel of the LORD killed a large number of the Assyrian army:

II Kings 19:35 - "That very night the angel of the LORD set out and struck down one hundred eighty-five thousand in the camp of the Assyrians; when morning dawned, they were all dead bodies" **(KJV)**.

- *Three Hebrews From Fiery Furnace*

Three friends of Daniel, Hananiah, Mishael, and Azariah were thrown into a fiery furnace by King Nebuchadnezzar but were saved by an angel.

Daniel 3:25 - "He said, 'Look! I see four men loosed *and* walking *about* in the midst of the fire without harm, and the appearance of the fourth is like a son of *the* gods'" **(NASB)**!

- *Preserved the Life Of Daniel*

An angel also preserved the life of Daniel in the lion's den:

Daniel 6:22 - "My God sent His angel and shut the lions' mouths so that they would not hurt me because I was found blameless before Him; and also before you, O king, I have done no wrong" **(RSV)**.

New Testament

In the speech of Stephen, angels are acknowledged as being involved when God gave the law. It was this Moses whom they rejected when they said, "Who made you a ruler and a judge?" It was Moses God now sent as both ruler and liberator through the angel who appeared to him in the bush. It was Moses who was with the congregation in the wilderness with the angel who spoke to our ancestors and to him at Mount Sinai. He received living oracles to give to us. You are the ones that received the law as ordained by angels, but you have not obeyed it.

References:

Acts 7:35 - "This Moses whom they refused, saying, Who made thee a ruler and a judge? The same did God send to be a ruler and a deliverer by the hand of the angel which appeared to him in the bush" **(KJV)**.

Acts 7:38 - "This is he, that was in the church in the wilderness with the angel which spake to him in the mount Sina, and with our fathers: who received the lively oracles to give unto us" **(KJV)**.

Acts 7:53 - "Who have received the law by the disposition of angels, and have not kept it" **(KJV)**.

Paul also spoke about this in his teachings in Galatians. What purpose then does the law serve? He emphasized it was added because of transgressions until the seed should come to whom the promise was made, and it was appointed through angels by the hand of a mediator.

> **Galatians 3:19** - "Wherefore then serveth the law? It was added because of transgressions, till the seed should come to whom the promise was made; and it was ordained by angels in the hand of a mediator" **(KJV)**.

The writer to the Hebrews concurred:

> **Hebrews 2:2** - "For if the word spoken by angels was stedfast, and every transgression and disobedience received a just recompence of reward" (KJV).

Angels seem to have a very close association with humans, perhaps closer than we realize, after examining biblical descriptions along with accounts of men and their experiences. In summary, angels described within the Bible, and from my personal experiences, we know that they are benevolent spirit beings that deliver messages from God, minister to humanity, and give assistance to the work and purpose of God on earth.

Origin of Angels

Angels Walk Among Us

CHAPTER 2
Angelic Organization

The Bible's revelation on the organization of God's host of angels is rather meager, but it is clear there does seem to be organization in the angelic world. They appear to be organized into various ranks and orders and positions. For example, Michael is called the Archangel or chief angel:

> **Jude 9** - "But even Michael, one of the mightiest of the angels, did not dare accuse the devil of blasphemy, but simply said, 'The Lord rebuke you'" **(NLT)**!

This took place when Michael was arguing with the devil about Moses' body.

> **Daniel 10:3** - "But the prince of the kingdom of Persia withstood me one and twenty days: but, lo, Michael, one of the chief princes, came to help me; and I remained there with the kings of Persia" **(KJV)**.

Ryrie states that additional ranks and orders are suggested by the terms used of angels (1987):

> **Ephesians 3:10** - "To the intent that now unto the principalities and powers in heavenly places might be known by the church the manifold wisdom of God" **(KJV)**.

Ephesians 6:12 - "For we wrestle not against flesh and blood, but against principalities, against powers, against the rulers of the darkness of this world, against spiritual wickedness in high places" **(KJV)**.

The Scriptures speak of the "assembly" and "council" of the angels:

Psalm 89:5 - "All heaven will praise your great wonders, LORD; myriads of angels will praise you for your faithfulness and He is far more awesome than all who surround his throne" **(NIV)**.

Psalm 89:7 - "The highest angelic powers stand in awe of God. He is far more awesome than all who surround his throne" **(NLT)**.

Some angels were organized for battle as described:

Revelation 12:7 - "Then there was war in heaven. Michael and his angels fought against the dragon and his angels" **(NLT)**.

Angels are also given a variety of classifications indicating organization and ranking:

Ephesians 3:10 - "So that through the church the wisdom of God in its rich variety might now be made known to the rulers and authorities in the heavenly places" **(RSV)**.

Ephesians 6:12 - "For our struggle is not against enemies of blood and flesh, but against the rulers, against the authorities, against the cosmic powers of this present darkness, against the spiritual forces of evil in the heavenly places" **(RSV)**.

Unquestionably, God has organized the elect angels (good angels) to be dispatched by God, and Satan has organized the evil angels to be dispatched by Satan.

A very important practical point for us emerges from this. Angels are organized; demons are organized; yet Christians, individually and in groups, may not feel that it is necessary that they be organized. When it comes to fighting evil forces, believers often feel that they can "go it alone" and expect victory without any substantial preparation and discipline. It is also true that when it comes to promoting good, believers often fall short of the best possible results because they do not make the effort to effectively organize, plan, and manage their good works (Ryrie, 1987).

This is further supported by Jude's statement regarding the angels who left their "domain" or "positions of authority" in Jude 6:

> **Jude 6** - "And angels who did not keep their own domain, but abandoned their proper abode, He has kept in eternal bonds under darkness for the judgment of the great day" **(NASB)**.

Angels who are governmental rulers.

> **Ephesians 6:12** - "For our struggle is not against flesh and blood, but against the rulers, against the powers, against the world forces of this darkness, against the spiritual forces of wickedness in the heavenly places. This refers to "ranking of fallen angels; rulers are "those who are first or high in rank"; powers are 'those invested with authority'; world-forces of this darkness "expresses the power or authority which they exercise over the world"; spiritual forces of wickedness describes

the wicked spirits, "expressing their character and nature" **(NASB)**.

Daniel 10:13 - "But the prince of the kingdom of Persia was withstanding me for twenty-one days; then behold, Michael, one of the chief princes, came to help me, for I had been left there with the kings of Persia" **(NASB)**.

This passage refers to the "prince of the kingdom of Persia" opposing Michael. This was not the king of Persia but rather a fallen angel under Satan's control; he was a demon of high rank, assigned by the chief of demons, Satan, to Persia as his special area of activity.

Revelation 12:7-9 - "And there was war in heaven: Michael and his angels fought against the dragon; and the dragon fought and his angels, And prevailed not; neither was their place found any more in heaven. And the great dragon was cast out, that old serpent, called the Devil, and Satan, which deceiveth the whole world: he was cast out into the earth, and his angels were cast out with him" **(KJV)**.

Angels who are highest ranking.

Michael is called the *archangel* in Jude 9 and *the great prince* in **Daniel 12**. Michael is the only angel designated *archangel* and may possibly be the only one of this rank. The mission of the *archangel* is protector of Israel and he is called "Michael your prince" in **Daniel 10**. There were chief princes, of whom Michael was one of the highest, ranking angels of God and possibly served as the highest ranking angel. Ruling Angels are also mentioned but no further details are given.

Daniel 10:13 - "But the prince of the kingdom of Persia was withstanding me for twenty-one days; then behold, Michael, one of the chief princes, came to help me, for I had been left there with the kings of Persia" **(NASB)**.

Ephesians 3:10 - "So that the manifold wisdom of God might now be made known through the church to the rulers and the authorities in the heavenly places" **(NASB)**.

Angels who are prominent individuals:

1. Michael

References:

Daniel 10:13 - "But the prince of the Persian kingdom resisted me twenty-one days. Then Michael, one of the chief princes, came to help me, because I was detained there with the king of Persia" **(NIV)**.

Daniel 12:1 - "At that time Michael, the great prince who protects your people, will arise. There will be a time of distress such as has not happened from the beginning of nations until then. But at that time your people, everyone whose name is found written in the book, will be delivered" **(NIV)**.

The name Michael means "who is like God?" and identifies the only one classified as an archangel in Scripture. The Bible tell us that Michael is described as the defender of Israel who will wage war on behalf of Israel against Satan and his hordes in the Tribulation. Michael also disputed with Satan about the body of Moses, but Michael refrained from judgment, leaving that to God:

> **Revelation 12:7-9** - "Then war broke out in heaven. Michael and his angels fought against the dragon, and the dragon and his angels fought back. But he was not strong enough, and they lost their place in heaven. The great dragon was hurled down, that ancient serpent called the devil, or Satan, who leads the whole world astray. He was hurled to the earth, and his angels with him" **(NIV)**.
>
> **Jude 9** - "But even the archangel Michael, when he was disputing with the devil about the body of Moses, did not himself dare to condemn him for slander but said, 'The Lord rebuke you'" **(NIV)**!

2. Gabriel

> *References:*
>
> **Daniel 9:21** - "While I was still in prayer, Gabriel, the man I had seen in the earlier vision, came to me in swift flight about the time of the evening sacrifice" **(NIV)**.
>
> **Luke 1:26** - "In the sixth month of Elizabeth's pregnancy, God sent the angel Gabriel to Nazareth, a town in Galilee" **(NIV)**.

The name Gabriel means "man of God", or "God is strong". Gabriel seems to be God's special messenger of His kingdom program in each of the four times he appears in the Bible record. He reveals and interprets God's purpose and program concerning Messiah and His kingdom to the prophets and people of Israel. In a highly significant passage, Gabriel explained the events of the seventy weeks for Israel:

> **Daniel 9:21-27** - "While I was still in prayer, Gabriel, the man I had seen in the earlier vision, came to me in swift flight about the time of the evening sacrifice. He instructed me and said to me, 'Daniel, I have now come to give you insight and understanding. As soon as you began to pray, a word went out, which I have come to tell you, for you are highly esteemed. Therefore, consider the word and understand the vision:' 'Seventy 'sevens' are decreed for your people and your holy city to finish transgression, to put an end to sin, to atone for wickedness, to bring in everlasting righteousness, to seal up vision and prophecy and to anoint the Most Holy Place. Know and understand this: From the time the word goes out to restore and rebuild Jerusalem until the Anointed One, the ruler, comes, there will be seven 'sevens,' and sixty-two 'sevens.' It will be rebuilt with streets and a trench, but in times of trouble. After the sixty-two 'sevens,' the Anointed One will be put to death and will have nothing. The people of the ruler who will come will destroy the city and the sanctuary. The end will come like a flood: War will continue until the end, and desolations have been decreed. He will confirm a covenant with many for one 'seven.' In the middle of the 'seven' he will put an end to sacrifice and offering. And at the temple he will set up an abomination that causes desolation, until the end that is decreed is poured out on him'" (**NIV**).

In **Luke 1**, Gabriel told Mary that the One born to her would be great and rule on the throne of David. In **Daniel 8** Gabriel explained to Daniel the succeeding kingdoms of Medo-Persia and Greece as well as the untimely death of Alexander the Great. Gabriel also announced the birth of John the Baptist to Zacharias in **Luke 1**.

> **Luke 1:26-27** - "In the sixth month of Elizabeth's pregnancy, God sent the angel Gabriel to Nazareth, a town in Galilee, to a virgin pledged to be married to a man named Joseph, a descendant of David. The virgin's name was Mary" **(NIV)**.

> **Daniel 8:15-16** - "While I, Daniel, was watching the vision and trying to understand it, there before me stood one who looked like a man. And I heard a man's voice from the Ulai calling, 'Gabriel, tell this man the meaning of the vision'" **(NIV)**.

3. Lucifer

References:

> **Isaiah 14:12** - "How you have fallen from heaven, morning star, son of the dawn! You have been cast down to the earth, you who once laid low the nations" **(NIV)**!

The name Lucifer means "shining one" or "star of the morning." We learn from the word of God that he may have been the wisest and most beautiful of all God's created beings. Lucifer was originally placed in a position of authority over the other angels, and over the cherubim surrounding the throne of God (Oehler, 1983).

Angels who are divine attendants.

Cherubims are of the highest order or class, created with indescribable powers and beauty. Their main purpose and activity could be summarized in this way: they are proclaimers and protectors of God's glorious presence, His sovereignty, and His holiness. God commanded a *cherubim* to stand guard at the gate of the Garden of Eden, preventing sinful man from entering:

> **Genesis 3:24** - "After he drove the man out, he placed on the east side of the Garden of Eden cherubim and a flaming sword flashing back and forth to guard the way to the tree of life" **(NIV)**.

The golden figures covering the mercy seat above the ark in the Holy of Holies, in **Exodus 25**, attended the glory of God in Ezekiel's vision in **Ezekiel 1**. Cherubims had an extraordinary appearance with four faces, that of a man, lion, ox, and eagle. They had four wings and feet like a calf, gleaming like burnished bronze. In **Ezekiel 1**, they attended the glory of God preparatory for judgment.

Seraphim, meaning "burning ones," are pictured in Ezekiel's vision surrounding the throne of God. In **Isaiah 6**, they are described as each having six wings and in their threefold proclamation of holiness. Isaiah further states it means "to recognize God as extremely, perfectly holy." Therefore, they praise and proclaim the perfect holiness of God. The *seraphim* also express the holiness of God in that they proclaim that man must be cleansed of sin's moral defilement before he can stand before God and serve Him.

> **Isaiah 6:2** - "Above him were seraphims, each with six wings: With two wings they covered their faces with two they covered their feet, and with two they were flying" **(NIV)**.
>
> **Isaiah 6:3** - "And they were calling to one another: "Holy, holy, holy is the LORD Almighty; the whole earth is full of his glory" **(NIV)**.

Regarding the governmental rulers in the angelic world, Ryrie described this as follows: (1987)

1. *Rulers or principalities:*

These words, used seven times by Paul, indicate an order of angel, both good and evil involved In governing the universe which God created:

References:

Romans 8:38 - "For I am convinced that neither death, nor life, nor angels, nor rulers, nor things present, nor things to come, nor powers" **(NRSV)**.

Ephesians 1:21 - "Far above all rule and authority and power and dominion, and above every name that is named, not only in this age but also in the age to come" **(NRSV)**.

Ephesians 3:10 - "So that through the church the wisdom of God in its rich variety might now be made known to the rulers and authorities in the heavenly places" **(NRSV)**.

Ephesians 6:12 - "For our struggle is not against enemies of blood and flesh, but against the rulers, against the authorities, against the cosmic powers of this present darkness, against the spiritual forces of evil in the heavenly places" **(NRSV)**.

Colossians 1:16 - "For in him all things in heaven and on earth were created, things visible and invisible, whether thrones or dominions or rulers or powers, all things have been created through him and for him" **(NIV)**.

Colossians 2:10 - "And you have come to fullness in him, who is the head of every ruler and authority" **(RSV)**.

Colossians 2:15 - "He disarmed the rulers and authorities and made a public example of them, triumphing over them in it" **(NRSV)**.

2. *Authority:*

Holy Scripture portrays this likely emphasizes the superhuman authority of angels and demons exercised in relation to the affairs of the world.

References:

Ephesians 2:2 - "In which you once lived, following the course of this world, following the ruler of the power of the air, the spirit that is now at work among those who are disobedient" **(NRSV)**.

I Peter 3:22 - "Who has gone into heaven and is at the right hand of God, with angel authorities, and powers made subject to him" **(KJV)**.

3. *Powers:*

In God's teaching, this word underscores the fact that angels and demons both have greater power than humans.

References:

II Peter 2:11 - "Whereas angels, which are greater in power and might, bring not railing accusation against them before the Lord " **(KJV)**.

Ephesians 1:21 - "Far above all principality, and power, and might, and dominion, and every name that is named, not only in this world, but also in that which is to come" (**KJV**).

I Peter 3:22 - "Who is gone into heaven, and is on the right hand of God; angels and authorities and powers being made subject unto him" (**KJV**).

4. Place of rule:

In one place demons are designated as world rulers of this darkness:

Ephesians 6:12 - "For our struggle is not against enemies of blood and flesh, but against the rulers, against the authorities, against the cosmic powers of this present darkness, against the spiritual forces of evil in the heavenly places" (**NRSV**).

5. Thrones or dominions.

This designation emphasizes the dignity and authority of angelic rulers in God's use of them in His government.

References:

Ephesians 1:21 - "Far above all rule and authority, power and dominion, and every name that is invoked, not only in the present age but also in the one to come" (**NIV**).

Colossians 1:16 - "For in him all things were created: things in heaven and on earth, visible and invisible, whether thrones or powers or rulers or authorities; all things have been created through him and for him" (**NIV**).

II Peter 2:10 - "This is especially true of those who follow the corrupt desire of the flesh and despise authority. Bold and arrogant, they are not afraid to heap abuse on celestial beings" **(NIV)**.

Jude 8 - "In the very same way, on the strength of their dreams these ungodly people pollute their own bodies, reject authority and heap abuse on celestial beings" **(NIV)**.

Some question remains whether the *Seraphim* and *Cherubim* are actually angels since they are never clearly identified as angels. However, due to the nature of angels, their service as superhuman servants of God and protector of God's Holy presence, this is the most logical place to classify them. It would be helpful to also consider Ryrie's explanation of these angelic beings (Ryrie 1987):

Cherubim:

Cherubims constitute another order of angels, evidently of high rank since Satan was described as a cherub:

Ezekiel 28:14 - "You were anointed as a guardian cherub, for so I ordained you. You were on the holy mount of God; you walked among the fiery stones" **(NIV)**.

Ezekiel 28:16 - "Through your widespread trade you were filled with violence, and you sinned. So I drove you in disgrace from the mount of God, and I expelled you, guardian cherub, from among the fiery stones" **(NIV)**.

The cherubim seem to function as guardians of the holiness of God, having guarded the way to the tree of life in the Garden of Eden:

Genesis 3:24 - "After he drove the man out, he placed on the east side of the Garden of Eden cherubim and a flaming sword flashing back and forth to guard the way to the tree of life" **(NIV)**.

The use of cherubim in the decoration of the inner sanctuary and temple may also indicate their mission as guardians:

Exodus 26:1 - "Make the tabernacle with ten curtains of finely twisted linen and blue, purple and scarlet yarn, with cherubim woven into them by a skilled worker" **(NIV)**.

I Kings 6:23-29 - "For the inner sanctuary he made a pair of cherubim out of olive wood, each ten cubits high. One wing of the first cherub was five cubits long, and the other wing five cubits - ten cubits from wing tip to wing tip. The second cherub also measured ten cubits, for the two cherubim were identical in size and shape. The height of each cherub was ten cubits. He placed the cherubim inside the innermost room of the temple, with their wings spread out. The wing of one cherub touched one wall, while the wing of the other touched the other wall, and their wings touched each other in the middle of the room. He overlaid the cherubim with gold. On the walls all around the temple, in both the inner and outer rooms, he carved cherubim, palm trees and open flowers" **(NIV)**.

Cherubim also bore the throne-chariot which Ezekiel saw in his vision:

Ezekiel 1:4-5 - "I looked, and I saw a windstorm coming out of the north, an immense cloud with flashing lightning and surrounded by brilliant light. The center of the fire looked like glowing metal, and in the fire was what looked like four living creatures. In appearance their form was human" (**NIV**).

Ezekiel 10:15-20 - "Then the cherubim rose upward. These were the living creatures I had seen by the Kebar River. When the cherubim moved, the wheels beside them moved; and when the cherubim spread their wings to rise from the ground, the wheels did not leave their side. When the cherubim stood still, they also stood still; and when the cherubim rose, they rose with them, because the spirit of the living creatures was in them. Then the glory of the LORD departed from over the threshold of the temple and stopped above the cherubim. While I watched, the cherubim spread their wings and rose from the ground, and as they went, the wheels went with them. They stopped at the entrance of the east gate of the LORD's house, and the glory of the God of Israel was above them. These were the living creatures I had seen beneath the God of Israel by the Kebar River, and I realized that they were cherubim" (**NIV**).

Some believe and identify the four living creatures of **Revelation 4** as cherubim but still others think these represent the attributes of God.

Revelation 4:6 - "Also in front of the throne there was what looked like a sea of glass, clear as crystal. In the center, around the throne, were four living creatures, and they were covered with eyes, in front and in back" (**NIV**).

Representations of the cherubim may also be a part of the millennial temple: (Ryrie, 1987).

Ezekiel 41:18-20 - "Were carved cherubim and palm trees. Palm trees alternated with cherubim. Each cherub had two faces: the face of a human being toward the palm tree on one side and the face of a lion toward the palm tree on the other. They were carved all around the whole temple. From the floor to the area above the entrance, cherubim and palm trees were carved on the wall of the main hall" **(NIV)**.

Seraphim:

All we know about this rank of angelic beings is found in:

Isaiah 6:2 - "Above him were seraphim, each with six wings: With two wings they covered their faces, with two they covered their feet, and with two they were flying" **(NIV)**.

Isaiah 6:6 - "Then one of the seraphim flew to me with a live coal in his hand, which he had taken with tongs from the altar" **(NIV)**.

Apparently the *seraphims* were an order similar to the *cherubim* and acted as attendants and guardians. Their physical description was that of a six-winged, human-like creature created to praise God and act as an agent of cleansing and purification. The word seraphim may be derived from a root meaning "to burn" or possibly from a root which means "to be noble" (Ryrie, 1987). There are 3 more classifications of angels:

Elect Angels: Paul speaks of the elect angels:

I Timothy 5:21 - "I charge you, in the sight of God and Christ Jesus and the elect angels, to keep these instructions without partiality, and to do nothing out of favoritism" **(NIV)**.

These are the holy angels who are somehow included in the elect purposes of God. These are angels who did not follow after Satan in his rebellion but remained faithful and are confirmed in their holy state in the service of the Lord. There is little revealed about their election, but there was a probationary period for the angelic world. As Chafer writes, "The fall of some angels is no more unanticipated by God than the fall of man. It may be implied, also that angels have passed a period of probation" (1993).

The Living Creatures: These are angelic creatures who seem to be involved with revealing the glory of the God of Israel in His omniscience, omnipotence, and omnipresence.

References:

Ezekiel 1:5 - "Also out of the midst thereof came the likeness of four living creatures. And this was their appearance; they had the likeness of a man" (**KJV**).

Revelation 4:6 - "And before the throne there was a sea of glass like unto crystal: and in the midst of the throne, and round about the throne, were four beasts full of eyes before and behind" (**KJV**).

Revelation 6:1 - "And I saw when the Lamb opened one of the seals, and I heard, as it were the noise of thunder, one of the four beasts saying, Come and see" (**KJV**).

Ezekiel 10:5 - "And the sound of the cherubims' wings was heard even to the outer court, as the voice of the Almighty God when he speaketh" (**KJV**).

Ezekiel 10:15 - "And the cherubims were lifted up. This is the living creature that I saw by the river of Chebar" (**KJV**).

Watchers: "Watchers" is an Aramaic word which means, vigilant, waking, and watchful. Daniel may infer this is a special type of angel. It seems to describe holy angels who are constantly vigilant to serve the Lord and who watch over the rulers of the world and the affairs of men (Jackson, 2019).

Daniel 4:13 - "In the visions I saw while lying in bed, I looked, and there before me was a holy one, a messenger, coming down from heaven" **(NIV)**.

Daniel 4:17 - "'The decision is announced by messengers, the holy ones declare the verdict, so that the living may know that the Most High is sovereign over all kingdoms on earth and gives them to anyone he wishes and sets over them the lowliest of people'" **(NIV)**.

Daniel 4:23 - "Your Majesty saw a holy one, a messenger, coming down from heaven and saying, 'Cut down the tree and destroy it, but leave the stump, bound with iron and bronze, in the grass of the field, while its roots remain in the ground. Let him be drenched with the dew of heaven; let him live with the wild animals, until seven times pass by for him'" **(NIV)**.

The added description, "a holy one" in **verse 13** may imply there are unholy watchers like demonic forces who are watching the affairs of men and seeking to influence and destroy.

The four faces of this creature may portray how God plans to bring salvation to man through His Son (Ryrie, 1987):

1. The face of the man suggests wisdom, compassion, intelligence and represents Christ's humanity as the Son of man, the special focus found in the gospel of Luke;

2. The face of a lion suggests kingly appearance and pictures Christ as King which is Matthew's emphasis;

3. The face of a bull or ox can portray a servant, the emphasis seen in Mark; and

4. The face of an eagle represents heavenly action and portrays the deity Christ, which is John's emphasis.

In Revelation, a number of angels are specifically associated with certain judgments that will be poured out on the earth. For example, the seven trumpets and the seven last plagues (**Revelation 8, 9** and **16**). In addition, some angels are assigned to perform specific functions given to them, at least in these last days. There is the angel who has power over fire:

Revelation 14:18 - "Still another angel, who had charge of the fire, came from the altar and called in a loud voice to him who had the sharp sickle, 'Take your sharp sickle and gather the clusters of grapes from the earth's vine, because its grapes are ripe'" **(NIV)**.

The angel of the waters is spoken about in:

Revelation 16:4 - "The third angel poured out his bowl on the rivers and springs of water, and they became blood" **(NIV)**.

The angel of the abyss who will bind Satan is mentioned in:

Revelation 20:1-2 - "And I saw an angel coming down out of heaven, having the key to the Abyss and holding in his hand a great chain. He seized the dragon, that ancient serpent, who is the devil, or Satan, and bound him for a thousand years" **(NIV)**.

In **Chapters 2 & 3** of **Revelation**, each of the seven letters to the seven churches is addressed to "the angel of the church of …". In addition, they are each seen to be in the right hand of Christ in the vision in the Bible verses:

> **Revelation 1:16** - "And he had in his right hand seven stars: and out of his mouth went a sharp two-edged sword: and his countenance was as the sun shineth in his strength" **(KJV)**.

> **Revelation 1:20** - "The mystery of the seven stars that you saw in my right hand and of the seven golden lampstands is this: The seven stars are the angels of the seven churches, and the seven lampstands are the seven churches" **(KJV)**.

However, since the term for angel means "messenger" and is also used of men, there is debate over whether these references refer to angelic beings or to the human leaders of the seven churches. It could also refer to a guardian angel over these churches or to those men who function in the capacity of teachers of the Word, like the human pastors or elders.

The Bible teaches that angels are well-organized in ranks. Though we are not told much about their classifications, we do know that there are various orders. Among the orders of angels are those who have authority over the elements. As further testimony that angels are indeed organized, we are told from Scripture that certain angels have authority over fire, water, and the pit, or the abyss. The Bible also says that an archangel or "chief angel" exists. This definitely suggests organization. Beyond this, we can only speculate or assume because it is not written.

Angelic Organization

Angels Walk Among Us

CHAPTER 3
Mission of Angels

The most basic characteristic of God's good angels is seen in the way they are described as ministering spirits and in the accounts of their many and varied activities of ministry described in Scripture. Essentially, they function as priestly messengers in the temple of God. From the account of their activities in the Bible, their service can be summarized as that of:

1. Worshippers of God

Isaiah 6:3 - "And one called out to another and said, "Holy, Holy, Holy, is the LORD of hosts, The whole earth is full of His glory" (**NASB**).

Revelation 4:8 - "And the four living creatures, each one of them having six wings, are full of eyes around and within; and day and night they do not cease to say, 'Holy, Holy, Holy is The Lord God, The Almighty, Who was, and Who is and Who is to Come'" (**NASB**).

2. As Messengers of God

Daniel 9:22 - "And he informed me, and talked with me, and said, O Daniel, I am now come forth to give thee skill and understanding" (**KJV**).

Luke 1:11, 26 - "And there appeared unto him an angel of the Lord standing on the right side of the altar of incense", and "And in the sixth month the angel Gabriel was sent from God unto a city of Galilee, named Nazareth" (**KJV**).

Luke 2:9 - "And, lo, the angel of the Lord came upon them, and the glory of the Lord shone round about them: and they were sore afraid" (**KJV**).

Revelation 1:1 - "The Revelation of Jesus Christ, which God gave unto him, to shew unto his servants things which must shortly come to pass; and he sent and signified it by his angel unto his servant John" (**KJV**).

3. As Soldiers in Spiritual Combat

Daniel 10:13 - "But the prince of the kingdom of Persia withstood me one and twenty days: but, lo, Michael, one of the chief princes, came to help me; and I remained there with the kings of Persia" (**KJV**).

Revelation 12:7 - "And there was war in heaven: Michael and his angels fought against the dragon; and the dragon fought and his angels" (**KJV**).

4. As Ministers to God's People:

Hebrews 1:14 - "Are they not all ministering spirits, sent forth to minister for them who shall be heirs of salvation?" (**KJV**).

Regarding the activity of angels as ministering spirits, Bushnell comments: The question may be asked, if we are not to worship the angels, or in any way pray to them, what is the value of the doctrine that they are "ministering spirits"

(1962)? In response, we can say that the Scriptural teaching in regard to the ministry of the angels is a beautiful enrichment of our conception of God's government of the world. As God's celestial servants who carry out His purposes, we may observe that their ministry falls into several different areas of service:

- *Service to God:*

In their service to God, angels are seen as attendants and guardians around His throne, waiting to serve Him and do His bidding regarding His purpose on earth:

> **Psalm 103:20** - "Praise the LORD, you angels, you mighty ones who carry out his plans, listening for each of his commands" **(NLT)**.
>
> **Isaiah 6:1** - "It was in the year King Uzziah died that I saw the Lord. He was sitting on a lofty throne, and the train of his robe filled the Temple" **(NIV)**.
>
> **Job 1:6** - "One day the members of the heavenly court came to present themselves before the LORD, and the Accuser, Satan, came with them" **(NLT)**.
>
> **Job 2:1** - "One day the members of the heavenly court came again to present themselves before the LORD, and the Accuser, Satan, came with them" **(NLT)**.
>
> **Revelation 5:11** - "Then I looked again, and I heard the voices of thousands and millions of angels around the throne and of the living beings and the elders" **(NLT)**.
>
> **Revelation 8:1** - "When the Lamb broke the seventh seal on the scroll, there was silence throughout heaven for about half an hour" **(NLT)**.

- *As Worshippers in Praise of Him:*

Isaiah 6:3 - "And one called to another and said: 'Holy, holy, holy is the LORD of hosts; the whole earth is full of his glory'" (**NRSV**).

Psalm 148:1-2 - "Praise the LORD! Praise the LORD from the heavens; praise him in the heights! Praise him, all his angels; praise him, all his host" (**NRSV**)!

Hebrews 1:6 - "And again, when he brings the firstborn into the world, he says, Let all God's angels worship him" (**NRSV**).

Revelation 5:12 - "Singing with full voice, Worthy is the Lamb that was slaughtered to receive power and wealth and wisdom and might and honor and glory and blessing" (**NRSV**)!

- *As Observers Who Rejoice Over What He Does:*

Job 38:6-7 - "On what were its bases sunk, or who laid its cornerstone when the morning stars sang together and all the heavenly beings shouted for joy" (**NRSV**)?

Luke 2:12-13 - "This will be a sign for you: you will find a child wrapped in bands of cloth and lying in a manger. And suddenly there was with the angel a multitude of the heavenly host, praising God and saying" (**NRSV**).

Luke 15:10 - "Just so, I tell you, there is joy in the presence of the angels of God over one sinner who repent" (**NRSV**).

- *As Soldiers in Battle with Satan:*

Revelation 12:7 - "Then war broke out in heaven. Michael and his angels fought against the dragon, and the dragon and his angels fought back" **(NIV)**.

- *As Instruments of His Judgments*

Revelation 7:1 - "And after these things I saw four angels standing on the four corners of the earth, holding the four winds of the earth, that the wind should not blow on the earth, nor on the sea, nor on any tree" **(KJV)**.

Revelation 8:2 - "And I saw the seven angels which stood before God; and to them were given seven trumpets" **(KJV)**.

- *In Service to Israel:*

In service to the nation of Israel, Michael, the archangel, seems to have a very important ministry as their guardian:

Daniel 10:13 - "But the prince of the kingdom of Persia withstood me one and twenty days: but, lo, Michael, one of the chief princes, came to help me; and I remained there with the kings of Persia" **(KJV)**.

Daniel 10:21 - "But I will shew thee that which is noted in the scripture of truth: and there is none that holdeth with me in these things, but Michael your prince" **(KJV)**.

Daniel 12:1 - "And at that time shall Michael stand up, the great prince which standeth for the children of thy people: and there shall be a time of trouble, such as never was since there was a nation even to that same time: and at that time thy people shall be delivered, every one that shall be found written in the book" **(KJV)**.

Jude 9 - "Yet Michael the archangel, when contending with the devil he disputed about the body of Moses, durst not bring against him a railing accusation, but said, The Lord rebuke thee" **(KJV)**.

- *In Service to Other Nations,
  They Watch Over Rulers and Nations:*

Daniel 4:17 - "This matter is by the decree of the watchers, and the demand by the word of the holy ones: to the intent that the living may know that the most High ruleth in the kingdom of men, and giveth it to whomsoever he will, and setteth up over it the basest of men" **(NIV)**.

Daniel 10:21 - "But I will shew thee that which is noted in the scripture of truth: and there is none that holdeth with me in these things, but Michael your prince" **(NIV)**.

Daniel 11:1 - "Also I in the first year of Darius the Mede, even I, stood to confirm and to strengthen him" **(NIV)**.

In the times of the Tribulation, angels will be the agents God uses to pour out His judgments in: **Revelation 8, 9,** and **16**.

- *In Service to Christ:*

With the plan of God centering in the person of His Son, Jesus Christ, angels will naturally perform many services for the Savior.

Birth of Jesus

They predicted it in:

Matthew 1:20 - "But while he thought on these things, behold, the angel of the LORD appeared unto him in a dream, saying, Joseph, thou son of David, fear not to take unto thee Mary thy wife: for that which is conceived in her is of the Holy Ghost" **(KJV)**.

The Bible says in **Luke 1:26-28** - "And in the sixth month the angel Gabriel was sent from God unto a city of Galilee, named Nazareth, To a virgin espoused to a man whose name was Joseph, of the house of David; and the virgin's name was Mary. And the angel came in unto her, and said, Hail, thou that art highly favored, the Lord is with thee: blessed art thou among women" **(KJV)**.

And then it was announced about His birth.

Luke 2:8-15 - "And there were in the same country shepherds abiding in the field, keeping watch over their flock by night. And, lo, the angel of the Lord came upon them, and the glory of the Lord shone round about them: and they were sore afraid. And the angel said unto them, Fear not: for, behold, I bring you good tidings of great joy, which shall be to all people. For unto you is born this day in the city of David a Savior, which is Christ the Lord. And this shall be a sign unto you; Ye shall find the babe wrapped in swaddling clothes, lying in a manger. And suddenly there was with the angel a multitude of the heavenly host praising God, and saying, Glory to God in the highest, and on earth peace, good will toward men. And it came to pass, as the angels were gone away from them into heaven, the shepherds said one to another, Let us now go even unto Bethlehem, and see this thing which is come to pass, which the Lord hath made known unto us" **(KJV)**.

An angel warned Joseph to take Mary and the baby Jesus and flee into Egypt.

> **Matthew 2:13-15** - "And when they were departed, behold, the angel of the Lord appeareth to Joseph in a dream, saying, Arise, and take the young child and his mother, and flee into Egypt, and be thou there until I bring thee word: for Herod will seek the young child to destroy him. When he arose, he took the young child and his mother by night, and departed into Egypt: And was there until the death of Herod: that it might be fulfilled which was spoken of the Lord by the prophet, saying, Out of Egypt have I called my son and an angel directed the family to return to Israel after Herod died" **(KJV)**.

> **Matthew 2:19-21** - "But when Herod was dead, behold, an angel of the Lord appeareth in a dream to Joseph in Egypt, Saying, Arise, and take the young child and his mother, and go into the land of Israel: for they are dead which sought the young child's life. And he arose, and took the young child and his mother, and came into the land of Israel" **(KJV)**.

His suffering

Angels ministered to the Lord after His temptation:

> **Matthew 4:11** - "Then the devil left Him; and behold, angels came and *began* to minister to Him" **(NASB)**.

> **Luke 22:43** - "And there appeared an angel unto him from heaven, strengthening him" **(KJV)**.

Jesus said He could have called a legion of angels who stood ready to come to His defense if He so desired.

Matthew 26:53 - "Thinkest thou that I cannot now pray to my Father, and he shall presently give me more than twelve legions of angels" **(KJV)**?

His resurrection

An angel descended from heaven and rolled away the stone from the tomb.

Matthew 28:1-2 - "In the end of the sabbath, as it began to dawn toward the first day of the week, came Mary Magdalene and the other Mary to see the sepulchre. And, behold, there was a great earthquake: for the angel of the Lord descended from heaven, and came and rolled back the stone from the door, and sat upon it" **(KJV)**.

Angels announced His resurrection to the women on Easter morning!

Matthew 28:5-6 - "And the angel answered and said unto the women, Fear not ye: for I know that ye seek Jesus, which was crucified. He is not here: for he is risen, as he said. Come, see the place where the Lord lay" **(KJV)**.

Luke 24:5-7 - "And as they were afraid, and bowed down their faces to the earth, they said unto them, Why seek ye the living among the dead? He is not here, but is risen: remember how he spake unto you when he was yet in Galilee, Saying, The Son of man must be delivered into the hands of sinful men, and be crucified, the third day rise again" **(KJV)**.

And angels were present at His ascension and gave instruction to the disciples:

> **Acts 1:10-11** - "And while they looked stedfastly toward heaven as he went up, behold, two men stood by them in white apparel; Which also said, Ye men of Galilee, why stand ye gazing up into heaven? this same Jesus, which is taken up from you into heaven, shall so come in like manner as ye have seen him go into heaven" **(KJV)**.

His coming again

The voice of the archangel will be heard at the translation of the church.

> **I Thessalonians 4:16** - "For the Lord himself shall descend from heaven with a shout, with the voice of the archangel, and with the trump of God: and the dead in Christ shall rise first" **(KJV)**.

Angels will accompany Him in His glorious return to earth.

> **Matthew 25:31** - "When the Son of man shall come in his glory, and all the holy angels with him, then shall he sit upon the throne of his glory" **(KJV)**.

> **II Thessalonians 1:7** - "And to you who are troubled rest with us, when the Lord Jesus shall be revealed from heaven with his mighty angels" **(KJV)**.

The angels will also separate the wheat from the tares at Christ's second coming:

> **Matthew 13:39-40** - "The enemy that sowed them is the devil; the harvest is the end of the world; and

the reapers are the angels. As therefore the tares are gathered and burned in the fire; so shall it be in the end of this world" **(KJV)**.

In Service to the Unrighteous:

Angels not only announce but also inflict judgment as shown in:

Genesis 19:13 - "Because we are going to destroy this place. The outcry to the LORD against its people is so great that he has sent us to destroy it" **(NIV)**.

Revelation 14:6-7 - "Then I saw another angel flying in midair, and he had the eternal gospel to proclaim to those who live on the earth - to every nation, tribe, language and people. He said in a loud voice, 'Fear God and give him glory, because the hour of his judgment has come. Worship him who made the heavens, the earth, the sea and the springs of water'" **(NIV)**.

Acts 12:23 - "Immediately, because Herod did not give praise to God, an angel of the Lord struck him down, and he was eaten by worms and died" **(KJV)**.

Revelation 16:1 - "Then I heard a loud voice from the temple saying to the seven angels, 'Go, pour out the seven bowls of God's wrath on the earth'" **(NIV)**.

The righteous and the unrighteous will be separated by angels:

Matthew 13:39-40 - "The enemy that sowed them is the devil; the harvest is the end of the world; and the reapers are the angels. As therefore the tares are gathered and burned in the fire; so shall it be in the end of this world" **(KJV)**.

In Service to the Church:

Hebrews 1:14 - "Are not all angels ministering spirits sent to serve those who will inherit salvation?" **(NIV)**.

Paul describes their ministry as "ministering spirits", sent out to render service for the sake of those who will inherit salvation. In this, however, Scripture points to a number of specific ministries angel have been involved in. They bring answers to prayer and help in bringing people to the Savior:

Acts 12:5-10 - "So Peter was kept in prison, but the church was earnestly praying to God for him. The night before Herod was to bring him to trial, Peter was sleeping between two soldiers, bound with two chains, and sentries stood guard at the entrance. Suddenly an angel of the Lord appeared and a light shone in the cell. He struck Peter on the side and woke him up. 'Quick, get up!' he said, and the chains fell off Peter's wrists. Then the angel said to him, 'Put on your clothes and sandals'. And Peter did so. 'Wrap your cloak around you and follow me,' the angel told him. Peter followed him out of the prison, but he had no idea that what the angel was doing was really happening; he thought he was seeing a vision. They passed the first and second guards and came to the iron gate leading to the city. It opened for them by itself, and they went through it. When they had walked the length of one street, suddenly the angel left him" **(NIV)**.

Acts 8:26 - "Now an angel of the Lord said to Philip, 'Go south to the road, the desert road, that goes down from Jerusalem to Gaza'"and (Acts 10:3), "One day at about three in the afternoon he had a vision. He distinctly saw an angel of God, who came to him and said, 'Cornelius'" **(NIV)**!

Acts 27:23-24 - "Last night an angel of the God to whom I belong and whom I serve stood beside me and said, 'Do not be afraid, Paul. You must stand trial before Caesar; and God has graciously given you the lives of all who sail with you'" **(NIV)**.

Angels may encourage in times of danger and desperation, and they care for God's people at the time of death.

Luke 16:22 - "The time came when the beggar died and the angels carried him to Abraham's side. The rich man also died and was buried" **(KJV)**.

In Service to the EVENTS Proclaimed by God:

Ryrie points out that angels appear to be unusually active when God sets plans and launches a new period of time in the sweep of history and then outlines for us (1987):

A. They Joined in Praise When the Earth Was Created:

Job 38:6-7 - "On what were its footings set, or who laid its cornerstone - while the morning stars sang together and all the angels shouted for joy" **(NIV)**?

B. They Were Involved in the Giving of the Mosaic Law:

Galatians 3:19 - "Why, then, was the law given at all? It was added because of transgressions until the Seed to whom the promise referred had come The law was given through angels and entrusted to a mediator" **(NIV)**; and

Hebrews 2:2 - "For since the message spoken through angels was binding, and every violation and disobedience received its just punishment" **(NIV)**.

C. They Were Active at the First Advent of Christ:

Matthew 1:20 - "But after he had considered this, an angel of the Lord appeared to him in a dream and said, 'Joseph son of David, do not be afraid to take Mary home as your wife, because what is conceived in her is from the Holy Spirit'" **(NIV)**.

Matthew 4:11 - "Then the devil left him, and angels came and attended him" **(NIV)**.

D. They Were Active During the Early Years of the Church;

Acts 8:26 - "Now an angel of the Lord said to Philip, 'Go south to the road, - the desert road - that goes down from Jerusalem to Gaza'" **(NIV)**.

Acts 10:3 - "One day at about three in the afternoon he had a vision. He distinctly saw an angel of God, who came to him and said, 'Cornelius!'" **(NIV)**.

Acts 10:7 - "When the angel who spoke to him had gone, Cornelius called two of his servants and a devout soldier who was one of his attendants" **(NIV)**.

Acts 12:11 - "Then Peter came to himself and said, 'Now I know without a doubt that the Lord has sent his angel and rescued me from Herod's clutches and from everything the Jewish people were hoping would happen'" (NIV).

E. They Will Be Involved in Events Surrounding the Second Advent of Christ.

Matthew 25:31 - "When the Son of Man comes in his glory, and all the angels with him, he will sit on his glorious throne" **(NIV)**.

Of course, the ministry of angels occurred in previous times, but the question naturally arises, especially in view of our present day fascination with angels, is there Scriptural evidence these varied ministries of angels continue to function in the present age of the church? Whether angels continue to function in all these ways throughout the present age is uncertain.

They did perform various documented ministries and may well continue to do so today, though we are not be aware of them. Of course, God is not obliged to use angels; He can do all these things directly. But seemingly, He chooses to employ the intermediate ministry of angels on many occasions.

Nevertheless, the believer recognizes that it is the Lord who does these things directly through using angels. Peter's testimony was that the Lord delivered him from prison although an angel was actually tasked by God to perform this deed:

Acts 12:7-10 - "Suddenly an angel of the Lord appeared and a light shone in the cell. He struck Peter on the side and woke him up. 'Quick, get up!' he said, and the chains fell off Peter's wrists. Then the angel said to him, 'Put on your clothes and sandals'. And Peter did so. 'Wrap your cloak around you and follow me,' the angel told him. Peter followed him out of the prison, but he had no idea that what the angel was doing was really happening; he thought he was seeing a vision. They passed the first and second guards and came to the iron gate leading to the city. It opened for them by itself, and they went through it. When they had walked the length of one street, suddenly the angel left him" **(NIV)**.

Acts 12:11 - "Then Peter came to himself and said, 'Now I know without a doubt that the Lord has sent his angel and rescued me from Herod's clutches and from everything the Jewish people were hoping would happen'" **(NIV)**.

Acts 12:17 - "Peter motioned with his hand for them to be quiet and described how the Lord had brought him out of prison. 'Tell James and the other brothers and sisters about this,' he said, and then he left for another place" **(NIV)**.

Hebrews 13:2 reads, "Do not neglect to show hospitality to strangers, for by this some have entertained angels without knowing it" **(NASB)**.

Genesis 18:1 - "The LORD appeared to Abraham near the great trees of Mamre while he was sitting at the entrance to his tent in the heat of the day" **(NIV)**.

He entertained angels without knowing it. Entertaining angels unawares brings to mind Abraham and Lot.

Genesis 19:1 - "The two angels arrived at Sodom in the evening, and Lot was sitting in the gateway of the city. When he saw them, he got up to meet them and bowed down with his face to the ground" **(NIV)**.

Even this statement does not prove angels function today as in Old and New Testament times. As Ryrie points out, the word "angel" may refer to celestial beings and Genesis 18 is an example of such entertaining or it may refer to a human being who is a messenger from God (1987).

James 2:25 - "In the same way, was not even Rahab the prostitute considered righteous for what she did when she gave lodging to the spies and sent them off in a different direction" **(NIV)**?

Perhaps no aspect of their ministry to man is more talked about than the idea of "a guardian angel." People often ask, "Does everyone have a guardian angel?" The concept that every person has a specific guardian angel is simply implied from the statement that angels do guard or protect us.

> **Psalm 91:11** - "For he will command his angels concerning you to guard you in all your ways" **(NIV)**.

But this passage is directed to those who make the Lord their refuge. The psalmist explained that no harm or disaster can befall those who have made the Lord their refuge because He has commissioned angels to care for them. Angels protect from physical harm and give believers strength to overcome difficulties, pictured here as wild lions and dangerous snakes.

> **Psalm 91:11-12** - "For he will command his angels concerning you to guard you in all your ways; they will lift you up in their hands, so that you will not strike your foot against a stone" **(NIV)**.

Satan, who tempted Christ several times, quoted:

> **Matthew 4:6** - "'If you are the Son of God,' he said, 'throw yourself down. For it is written:' "He will command his angels concerning you, and they will lift you up in their hands, so that you will not strike your foot against a stone'" **(NIV)**.

Some would claim that this Old Testament passage should not be applied in modern times, but:

> **Hebrews 1:14** - "Are they not all ministering spirits, sent forth to minister for them who shall be heirs of salvation" **(KJV)**?

The author of Hebrews does not seem to draw that distinction. That they are ministering spirits who minister to the saints is presented as a general truth of the Bible and should not be restricted to Biblical times.

Yes, it is comforting to know that God may protect, provide, and encourage us through His angels, but does this truth always guarantee such deliverance and protection to us? We should never presume on this provision of God. So having considered the various ways angels minister, we should keep in mind that God does not always deliver us from danger or supply our needs in miraculous ways by His direct intervention or by angels. Considering His own sovereign and wise purposes within God's plan, the opposite is sometimes His will. Life clearly illustrates and Scripture declares:

> **Hebrews 11:36-40** - "And others had trial of cruel mockings and scourgings, yea, moreover of bonds and imprisonment: They were stoned, they were sawn asunder, were tempted, were slain with the sword: they wandered about in sheepskins and goatskins; being destitute, afflicted, tormented; Of whom the world was not worthy: they wandered in deserts, and in mountains, and in dens and caves of the earth. And these all, having obtained a good report through faith, received not the promise: God having provided some better thing for us, that they without us should not be made perfect" **(KJV)**.

Just as people usually do not think of the punitive ministry of God's angels, so people, in their popular ideas about angels, often ignore the Scripture's teaching about the deception of Satan's evil angels. The truth regarding Satan's angels also needs to be kept in view.

> **II Corinthians 11:14-15** - "And no marvel; for Satan himself is transformed into an angel of light.

Therefore it is no great thing if his ministers also be transformed as the ministers of righteousness; whose end shall be according to their works" **(KJV)**.

The fact that society is ignorant of this is not without reason. The reason lies in Satan's deception and in the emptiness of man's heart as he continues to seek answers apart from God and Scripture's revelation of God and apart from His plan of salvation in Christ.

Satan is an arch deceiver and antagonist to God, to the church, and to mankind as a whole, and certainly the master of disguise. Society's current enchantment with angels is a product of his masquerade as an angel of light along with his evil angels who also disguise themselves in keeping with his plans and purposes. When you investigate what is being written in books and taught in seminars, you will find volumes of publications and teachings filled with what is nothing less than pure demonic deception.

Each angel has a mission on earth. God relies on his messengers to serve mankind. Throughout church history, angels have played a vital role in the Christian understanding of God's involvement in creation, in the affairs of humanity, in His plan of salvation in Christ, and ultimately in the consummation of history.

Mission of Angels

Angels Walk Among Us

CHAPTER 4
Names of Angels

There are only five angels named in the King James Version of the Bible: Abaddon (Apollyon), Lucifer/Satan, (Beelzeubub/Beelzebul) Gabriel, and Michael. Three are fallen angels, and two serve God. I will start with the names of the three fallen angels. But before I do, I want to explain why I have not used many of the other names that have been circulated for centuries. So, I am inserting the following paragraphs (off topic) in an effort to explain why I am using only five names in this chapter.

The biblical Apocrypha denotes the collection of apocryphal ancient books found in some editions of the bible in a separate section between the Old and New Testaments or as an appendix after the New Testament. Some Christian churches include some or all of the same texts within the body of their version of the Old Testament. The Westminster Confession of Faith excluded the Apocrypha from the canon, believing it was not of divine inspiration, is no authority in God's church on earth, therefore should not be a part of the canon of the Scripture. The Apocrypha section was then omitted in most modern editions of the Bible and reprintings of the King James Bible. For purposes of this writing, no reference is made to the Apocrypha to extract names of angels from it, although it mentions many (Metzger, 1977).

The Apocrypha contains 14 booklets and in those booklets are the names of many other angels, namely Raphal which was thought to be the 4th archangel. I have chosen rather to believe by the actions of Jesus Christ and the apostles wherein no reference is made to the apocryphal books.

Most Christians have regarded the authority of those books as secondary to that of the 39 books of the Old Testament and so have I.

- Lucifer/Satan

The Bible refers to him fifty-two times as "Satan" (adversary or opposer) and thirty-five times as the "Devil" (accuser or slanderer). Lucifer is thought to be the original name for the devil and originally possessed a high place in heaven. This name reflects not the present character of Satan but his original created purpose and character:

> **Isaiah 14:12** - "How you have fallen from heaven, morning star, son of the dawn! You have been cast down to the earth, you who once laid low the nations" **(NIV)**!

Perhaps the highest above all angels, but was cast down because of his desire to rise above God.

The name Lucifer means bearer of light. The name should have reflected his purpose to bear the light of God since angels were created as messengers of God. Lucifer could have been a light bearer to Jesus himself who is the true Light, which lighteth every man that cometh into the world:

> **John 1:9** - "The true light that gives light to everyone was coming into the world" **(NIV)**.

Satan is the adversary of God and mankind. He is the fallen angel, the devil, who rebelled against God and is mentioned more often in Scripture than all other angels combined. Out of twenty-nine references in the Gospels, Jesus spoke of Satan twenty-five times" (Blanchard, 2007).

- He is "the prince of demons"

II Corinthians 4:4 - "In whose case the god of this world has blinded the minds of the unbelieving so that they might not see the light of the gospel of the glory of Christ, who is the image of God" **(NASB)**.

He is in charge of the whole world order that rejects the Creator and substitutes the creature. Other titles include:

- "The evil one"

Matthew 12:24 - "But when the Pharisees heard this, they said, 'This man casts out demons only by Beelzebul the ruler of the demons'" **(NASB)**.

- He is the "undisputed ruler" of a host of evil spirits that inhabit the heavenlies as surely as humanity inhabits planet earth:

- He is "the ruler of this world"

John 12:31 - "Now judgment is upon this world; now the ruler of this world will be cast out" **(KJV)**.

- He is "the prince of the power of the air"

- He is always exercising massive authority in the ordered system of things opposed to God.

Ephesians 2:2 - "Wherein in time past ye walked according to the course of this world, according to the prince of the power of the air, the spirit that now worketh in the children of disobedience" **(KJV)**.

- He is "the god of this world"

John 17:15 - "I do not ask You to take them out of the world, but to keep them from the evil one" **(NASB)**.

- "A roaring lion"

I Peter 5:8 - "Be of sober spirit, be on the alert. Your adversary, the devil, prowls around like a roaring lion, seeking someone to devour" **(NASB)**.

- "Abaddon" ("destroyer")

Revelation 9:11 - "They have as king over them, the angel of the abyss; his name in Hebrew is Abaddon, and in the Greek he has the name Apollyon" **(NASB)**.

- "A great red dragon"

Revelations 12:3 - "Then another sign appeared in heaven: and behold, a great red dragon having seven heads and ten horns, and on his heads were seven diadems" **(NASB)**.

- "That ancient serpent"

Revelations 12:9 - "And the great dragon was thrown down, the serpent of old who is called the devil and Satan, who deceives the whole world; he was thrown down to the earth, and his angels were thrown down with him" **(NASB)**.

He's mentioned thirty-five times in the New Testament:

Matthew 4:10 - "Then Jesus said to him, 'Go, Satan'! For it is written, 'You shall worship the Lord your God, and serve Him only'" **(NASB)**.

Mark 1:13 - "And He was in the wilderness forty days being tempted by Satan; and He was with the wild beasts, and the angels were ministering to Him" **(NASB)**.

Luke 22:3 - "And Satan entered into Judas who was called Iscariot, belonging to the number of the twelve" **(NASB)**.

Romans 16:20 - "The God of peace will soon crush Satan under your feet. The grace of our Lord Jesus be with you" **(NASB)**.

II Corinthians 11:14 - "No wonder, for even Satan disguises himself as an angel of light" **(NASB)**.

We have been given a terrifying picture of Satan's influence, not merely of some of kind of vague influence but of an immensely, amazingly clever, intrinsically evil and destructive person, the ruler and leader of a host of lesser spirits completely under his control.

- Abaddon/Apollyon

The name Abaddon or Apollyon appears in:

Revelation 9:11 - "They have as king over them, the angel of the abyss; his name in Hebrew is Abaddon, and in the Greek he has the name Apollyon" **(KJV)**.

In Hebrew, the name "Abaddon" means "place of destruction"; the Greek title "Apollyon" literally means "The Destroyer"

(Got Questions Ministries, 2017). Abaddon/Apollyon is often used as another name for Satan. However, Scripture seems to make a distinction between the two. Abaddon/Apollyon is likely one of Satan's underlings, a destroying demon and one of the "rulers," "authorities," and "powers" mentioned in:

> **Ephesians 6:12** - "For we wrestle not against flesh and blood, but against principalities, against powers, against the rulers of the darkness of this world, against spiritual wickedness in high places" **(KJV)**.
>
> **Psalm 88:11** - "Will Your lovingkindness be declared in the grave, Your faithfulness in Abaddon" **(NASB)**?
>
> **Proverbs 15:11** - "Sheol and Abaddon lie open before the Lord, How much more the hearts of men!" **(NASB)**.
>
> **Proverbs 27:20** - "Sheol and Abaddon are never satisfied, Nor are the eyes of man ever satisfied" **(NASB)**.

- Beelzeubub/Beelzebul

Beelzebub is the Greek form of the name Baal-zebub, a pagan Philistine god worshiped in the ancient Philistine city of Ekron during the Old Testament times. It is a term signifying "the lord of flies" in:

> **II Kings 1:2** - "And Ahaziah fell down through a lattice in his upper chamber that was in Samaria, and was sick: and he sent messengers, and said unto them, Go, enquire of Baalzebub the god of Ekron whether I shall recover of this disease" **(NASB)**.
>
> **II Kings 1:16** - "Then he said to him, 'Thus says the LORD, Because you have sent messengers to inquire of Baal-zebub, the god of Ekron, is it because there

is no God in Israel to inquire of His word-therefore you shall not come down from the bed where you have gone up, but shall surely die'" **(NASB)**.

Beelzeubub or Beelzebul means "Lord of the flies". Golden images of flies have been discovered at archaeological excavations in ancient Philistine locations. After the time of the Philistines, the Jews changed the name to "Beelzeboul," as used in the Greek New Testament, meaning "lord of dung." This name referenced the god of the fly that was worshiped to receive healing from the injuries of that insect. Some biblical scholars believe Beelzebub was also known as the "god of filth," and later became a name spoken with contempt and mockery by the Pharisees. As a result, Beelzeboul was a particularly despicable and vile deity and his name was used by Jews as another name for Satan (Slick, 2013).

> **Revelation 9:11** states, "And they had a king over them, which is the angel of the bottomless pit, whose name in the Hebrew tongue is Abaddon, but in the Greek tongue hath his name Apollyon" **(KJV)**.

It appears that there is another reference or name of Satan in the New Testament. The word appears as a name of a false god in the Old Testament:

> **Matthew 12:24** - "But when the Pharisees heard this, they said, 'This man casts out demons only by Beelzebul the ruler of the demons'" **(NASB)**.

> **Matthew 10:25** - "It is enough for the disciple that he become like his teacher, and the slave like his master. If they have called the head of the house Beelzebul, how much more will they malign the members of his household!" **(NASB)**.

Mark 3:22 - "The scribes who came down from Jerusalem were saying, 'He is possessed by Beelzebul,' and 'He casts out the demons by the ruler of the demon'" **(NASB)**.

Luke 11:15 - "But some of them said, 'He casts out demons by Beelzebul, the ruler of the demons'" **(NASB)**.

Matthew 12:22 - "Then was brought unto him one possessed with a devil, blind, and dumb: and he healed him, insomuch that the blind and dumb both spake and saw" **(KJV)**.

Matthew 12:23-24 - "And all the people were amazed, and said, Is not this the son of David? But when the Pharisees heard it, they said, this fellow doth not cast out devils, but by Beelzebub the prince of the devils" **(KJV)**.

It is remarkable that the Pharisees reacted to this incredible miracle by Jesus in the very opposite way of that of the multitude, who realized that Jesus was from God. In fact, it was an admission by the Pharisees that Jesus did work miracles and performed deeds beyond the reach of any unaided human power; however, they attributed this power to Beelzebub instead of God. The Pharisees should have known that the devil cannot do works of pure goodness. However, in their self-absorbed pride, these Pharisees knew that if the teachings of Jesus should prevail among the people, their influence over them was at an end. So, the miracle they did not deny, but instead attributed it to a hellish infernal power, "Beelzebub the prince of the demons" (Dickason, 1997).

The point Jesus is making to us today is that, if people are calling Him Satan, as did the Pharisees of His time, they would surely call His disciples the same. In John, Jesus declares:

John 15:18-21 - "If the world hates you, keep in mind that it hated me first. If you belonged to the world, it would love you as its own. As it is, you do not belong to the world, but I have chosen you out of the world. That is why the world hates you. Remember what I told you: 'A servant is not greater than his master.' If they persecuted me, they will persecute you also. If they obeyed my teaching, they will obey yours also. They will treat you this way because of my name, for they do not know the one who sent me" **(NIV)**.

THE THREE ARCHANGELS

The Bible has revealed the proper names of only three Angels, all of whom belong to the Choir of the Archangels. The names are well known to all, namely: Michael, Gabriel, and Lucifer.

THE ARCHANGEL GABRIEL

Even though Gabriel means "man of God."; the name of Jesus surpasses the name of Gabriel. Whereas Gabriel is the "man of God," Jesus is "God." He appears to be one who carries messages. He is an Archangel who appeared to Daniel as a man and gave him the meaning of a vision. In the New Testament, he appeared to Zechariah who was serving in the temple in order to announce the birth of John the Baptist. Six months later he appeared to Mary, informing her that she would be the mother of Jesus.

Daniel 8:16 - "And I heard the voice of a man between the banks of Ulai, and he called out and said, 'Gabriel, give this man an understanding of the vision'" **(NASB)**.

Daniel 9:21 - "While I was still speaking in prayer, then the man Gabriel, whom I had seen in the vision previously, came to me in my extreme weariness about the time of the evening offering" (NIV).

Luke 1:26 - "Now in the sixth month the angel Gabriel was sent from God to a city in Galilee called Nazareth" **(KJV)**.

Practically all the missions and manifestations of this Archangel are closely connected with the coming of the Messiah. The most accurate prophecy regarding the time of the coming of Christ was made by Gabriel through the prophet Daniel. Immediately before the coming of Christ we meet the Archangel Gabriel in the temple of Jerusalem, announcing to Zachary the birth of a son, John the Baptist, the precursor of Christ:

Luke 1:19 - "And the angel answering said unto him, 'I am Gabriel, that stand in the presence of God; and am sent to speak unto thee, and to shew thee these glad tidings'" **(KJV)**.

The greatest and by far the most joyful message ever committed to an Angel from the beginning of time, was the one brought by the Archangel Gabriel to Mary, announcing to her the Incarnation of the Word of God and the birth of Christ, the Savior of mankind. Mary was the single witness to Gabriel and this heavenly message, helping us to further understand the delicate mission of Gabriel in God's work of human redemption.

Gabriel greets Mary, an earthly child of God, with great respect and deference as a prince might greet his queen. It is the first time that a prince of the court of heaven greets an earthly child of God. This mission of Gabriel ushers in the beginning of a new covenant and fulfills God's promises to His people: The Angel Gabriel was sent from God into a city of Galilee, called Nazareth, to a virgin named Mary espoused to a man, whose name was Joseph, of the house of David.

Gabriel began to converse with Mary and made this proclamation in **Luke 1:28** - "Hail, thou that art highly favoured, the Lord is with thee: blessed art thou among women" **(KJV)**. Gabriel calms Mary's reaction of surprise at both his appearance and especially at his "manner of salutation." He must set aside Mary's puritanical thoughts of rigid morality and obtain her consent to become the mother of the Son of God. Gabriel nobly fulfills this task in **Luke 1:30** - "And the angel said unto her, Fear not, Mary: for thou hast found favour with God" **(KJV)**. Gabriel calls her by her own name in order to inspire confidence and to show affection and kindness in her state of anxiety. The great message is presented to her as a decree of the Most High God, a thing ordained in the eternal decree of the Incarnation, predicted centuries before by the prophets, and announced now to her as an imminent event depending on her consent:

> **Luke 1:31-33** - "Behold thou shalt conceive in thy womb, and shalt bring forth a son, and thou shalt call his name Jesus. He shall be great, and shall be called the Son of the Most High; and the Lord God shall give unto him the throne of David his father and he shall reign in the house of Jacob for ever. And of his kingdom there shall be no end" **(KJV)**.

From these words of the Angel, it became very evident to Mary that her son was to be the promised Messiah, the Son of David. But she did not know how to reconcile her vow of virginity with the promised motherhood, hence her question:

Luke 1:34 - "Then said Mary unto the angel, How shall this be, seeing I know not a man? "Gabriel's reply shows that God wanted to respect Mary's vow of virginity and thus make her a mother without a human father, in a miraculous way" (**KJV**).

Luke 1:35 - "And the angel answered and said unto her, The Holy Ghost shall come upon thee, and the power of the Highest shall overshadow thee: therefore, also that holy thing which shall be born of thee shall be called the Son of God" (**KJV**).

As a last word of encouragement and, at the same time, a most gratifying message, the Archangel reveals to Mary that her elderly and barren cousin Elizabeth is now an expectant mother in her sixth month of pregnancy. This final argument was offered in order:

Luke 1:37 - "For with God nothing shall be impossible" (**KJV**).

Mary, unshaken in her profound humility, replied: "Behold the handmaid of the Lord; be it done to me according to thy word." This reply was Mary's consent, a consent awaited by heaven and earth. The Archangel Gabriel departed from Mary to bring to all the Angels the glorious news of the announcement.

It seems likely that Gabriel was given special charge of the family of Nazareth. He was probably the Angel who brought good tidings of great joy to the shepherds keeping night watches over their flock, the night that Christ was born in Bethlehem. We notice on this occasion that Gabriel first calms their fear and surprise, as he had done when he delivered his message to Mary:

> **Luke 2:10-11** - "And the angel said unto them, Fear not: for, behold, I bring you good tidings of great joy, which shall be to all people. For unto you is born this day in the city of David a Saviour, which is Christ the Lord" **(KJV)**.

Gabriel the Archangel was most likely the messenger of such good tidings, who had promised them through the prophet Daniel, and announced them to Mary. Having delivered the joyful message, Gabriel is joined suddenly by a vast multitude of the heavenly hosts, singing, celebrating, and praising God in anticipation for the hope of human redemption.

> **Luke 2:13-14** - "And suddenly there was with the Angel a multitude of the heavenly army, praising God, and saying: Glory to God in the highest, and on earth peace to men of good will" **(KJV)**.

Gabriel's duties towards the Messiah did not come to an end with the birth of Jesus. Gabriel was most likely the angel who warned Joseph in his sleep while in Bethlehem.

> **Matthew 2:20** - "Saying, Arise, and take the young child and his mother, and go into the land of Israel: for they are dead which sought the young child's life" **(KJV)**.

After the death of Herod, the angel appeared to Joseph once again in Egypt to instruct him to bring the child and his mother back into the land of Israel.

Gabriel who is "the strength of God" probably was the angel mentioned by Luke, in his narrative of Christ's agony in the garden:

> **Luke 22:43** - "And there appeared to him an angel from heaven, strengthening him" **(KJV)**.

It seems likely the same angel who announced His coming to both the Old and New Testament and who witnessed the Savior's agony would also be the first to announce to the world that our Savior is resurrected , and triumph over sin and death on Easter morning is His:

> **Matthew 28:2-3** - "An Angel of the Lord descended from heaven, and coming rolled back the stone, and sat upon it. And his countenance was as lightning, and his raiment as snow" **(KJV)**.

Gabriel, who helped to prepare man for the work of redemption is most likely to be among the angels who will be harvesting "the dead who are in Christ" and who will be sent out to harvest the elect from the four corners of the earth. The divine commandment to the dead to rise again will be announced by the trumpet of God or the voice of the Archangel by the power of Almighty God.

Appearances of Gabriel

Gabriel is the messenger angel of God, usually sent from God to man with special messages.

To Whom Gabriel was sent - Scripture Reference:

- Daniel

> **Daniel 8:16** - "And I heard a man's voice from the Ulai calling, 'Gabriel, tell this man the meaning of the vision'" **(NIV)**.

> **Daniel 9:21** - "While I was still in prayer, Gabriel, the man I had seen in the earlier vision, came to me in swift flight about the time of the evening sacrifice" **(NIV)**.

Daniel 9:26 - "After the sixty-two 'sevens,' the Anointed One will be put to death and will have nothing. The people of the ruler who will come will destroy the city and the sanctuary. The end will come like a flood: War will continue until the end, and desolations have been decreed" **(NIV)**.

- Zacharias

Luke 1:11 - "Then an angel of the Lord appeared to him, standing at the right side of the altar of incense" **(NIV)**.

Luke 1:19 - "The angel said to him, 'I am Gabriel. I stand in the presence of God, and I have been sent to speak to you and to tell you this good news'" **(NIV)**.

- Mary

Luke 1:26-27 - "In the sixth month of Elizabeth's pregnancy, God sent the angel Gabriel to Nazareth, a town in Galilee, to a virgin pledged to be married to a man named Joseph, a descendant of David. The virgin's name was Mary" **(NIV)**.

- Joseph

Matthew 1:20 - "But after he had considered this, an angel of the Lord appeared to him in a dream and said, "Joseph son of David, do not be afraid to take Mary home as your wife, because what is conceived in her is from the Holy Spirit" **(NIV)**.

Matthew 2:13 - "When they had gone, an angel of the Lord appeared to Joseph in a dream. 'Get up,' he said, 'take the child and his mother and escape to

Egypt. Stay there until I tell you, for Herod is going to search for the child to kill him'" **(NIV)**.

Matthew 2:19 - "After Herod died, an angel of the Lord appeared in a dream to Joseph in Egypt" **(NIV)**.

- Jesus in Gethsemane

Luke 22:43 - "An angel from heaven appeared to him and strengthened him" **(NIV)**.

- The apostles in prison

Acts 5:19 - "But during the night an angel of the Lord opened the doors of the jail and brought them out" **(NIV)**.

- Philip

Acts 8:26 - "Now an angel of the Lord said to Philip, 'Go south to the road—the desert road—that goes down from Jerusalem to Gaza'" **(NIV)**.

- Peter

Acts 12:7 - "Suddenly an angel of the Lord appeared and a light shone in the cell. He struck Peter on the side and woke him up. 'Quick, get up!' he said, and the chains fell off Peter's wrists" **(NIV)**.

- Herod

Acts 12:23 - "Immediately, because Herod did not give praise to God, an angel of the Lord struck him down, and he was eaten by worms and died" **(NIV)**.

- Paul

Acts 27:23 - "Last night an angel of the God to whom I belong and whom I serve stood beside me" **(NIV)**.

- John

Revelation 22:8 - "I, John, am the one who heard and saw these things. And when I had heard and seen them, I fell down to worship at the feet of the angel who had been showing them to me" **(NASB)**.

THE ARCHANGEL MICHAEL

The second angel named in Scripture is the most powerful and is usually related to both Israel and the resurrection. He is described as the archangel **(Jude 9)**, meaning he is the highest in the order of God's angels. His name means "who is like the Lord?" which emphasizes his godly character. Once again this angelic name, too, falls short of the Lord Jesus Christ, as did Gabriel.

According to Oehler, "this name: Michael, who is as God?, of the prince of the Angels does not imply merely a humble acknowledgment on the part of the angel, but it is rather an actual assertion concerning the Angel himself. The name thus expresses the irresistibility of him to whom God gives the power to execute His commands" (1983).

Daniel 10:13 - "But the prince of the kingdom of Persia was withstanding me for twenty-one days; then behold, Michael, one of the chief princes, came to help me, for I had been left there with the kings of Persia" **(NASB)**.

Revelation 12:7-8 - "And there was war in heaven, Michael and his angels waging war with the dragon. The dragon and his angels waged war, and they were not strong enough, and there was no longer a place found for them in heaven" **(NASB)**.

The proper name of one of the great archangels, Michael, appears for the first time in the book of the prophet Daniel. He is called Michael, one of the chief princes, and called great prince in:

Daniel 12:1 - "At that time shall Michael rise up, the great prince, who standeth for the children of thy people" **(KJV)**.

The name "Archangel" is given to Michael again as shown in:

Jude 9 - "Yet Michael the archangel, when contending with the devil he disputed about the body of Moses, durst not bring against him a railing accusation, but said, The Lord rebuke thee" **(KJV)**.

We see that the two angels Gabriel and Michael I have mentioned are spoken of as archangels and were entrusted with extraordinary missions. Michael is the only one to whom the Bible applies the title of Archangel, but there is good reason to believe he may be the very highest of all the angels.

Michael is indeed a prince of the heavenly hosts, belonging to an order of ministering spirits namely Principalities, Archangels, and Angels. This is sufficiently explained by the power granted him by God and not necessarily by superiority of nature. We believe that a power of that sort would not be conferred upon Seraphim and Cherubim who are living near the throne of God, but rather to an angel or archangel.

Hebrews 1:14 - "Are not all angels ministering spirits sent to serve those who will inherit salvation" **(NIV)**?

Michael has always been the warrior angel, fighting first Satan and his demons from the beginning, and in the course of time, all the enemies of God's own people. As of old, and so today, Michael is the great defender of the Church of Christ on earth and stands for the children of God's people. This mysterious term "Angel of the Lord" is referred to in various books of the Old Testament as acting in the name of God himself, and is often honored and accepted as God would be. We can reason that Archangel Michael has always been God's personal emissary and protector of His people. He represented God as a heavenly prince and was protector of God's own people against both human and spiritual enemies (Dickason, 1997).

Michael had defended and protected God's children in the spirit world, and provided the same protection to the human children of God here on earth. Satan had established his rule of the hostile pagan nations which surrounded and threatened God's children and introduced new forms of seduction and rebellion among the children of men. As long as Satan persists in his attacks, the heavenly champion, the Prince of the heavenly hosts will continue to crush those attacks with the war cry of old: "Who is as God?" In the Old Testament, Michael is the Angel of the Lord who became the national Guardian Angel of the Israelites.

At times, especially in the book of Exodus, this "Angel of the Lord" is called simply, the Lord; as for example in this passage:

Exodus 13:21 - "By day the Lord went ahead of them in a pillar of cloud to guide them on their way and by night in a pillar of fire to give them light, so that they could travel by day or night" **(NIV)**.

He who is called "the Lord" in this passage, is mentioned again in the same capacity as the Angel of God in the following passage:

> **Exodus 14:19** - "Then the angel of God, who had been traveling in front of Israel's army, withdrew and went behind them. The pillar of cloud also moved from in front and stood behind them" **(NIV)**.

This very clever military-like maneuver clearly shows the strategy of the Prince of heavenly hosts. As the national Guardian Angel of the Israelites and God's special protector to His people, Michael is introduced with words which reveal the great divine love and attention of the Lord, together with man's duties towards Guardian Angels in general:

> **Exodus 23:20-23** - "Behold, I send an Angel before thee, to keep thee in the way, and to bring thee into the place which I have prepared. Beware of him, and obey his voice, provoke him not; for he will not pardon your transgressions: for my name is in him. But if thou shalt indeed obey his voice, and do all that I speak; then I will be an enemy unto thine enemies, and an adversary unto thine adversaries. For mine Angel shall go before thee, and bring thee in unto the Amorites, and the Hittites, and the Perizzites, and the Canaanites, the Hivites, and the Jebusites: and I will cut them off" **(KJV)**.

Appearances of Michael

- To Whom Michael was sent – Scripture Reference

> **Daniel 10:21** - "However, I will tell you what is inscribed in the writing of truth. Yet there is no one who stands firmly with me against these forces except Michael your prince" **(NASB)**.

Daniel 12:1 - "Now at that time Michael, the great prince who stands guard over the sons of your people, will arise. And there will be a time of distress such as never occurred since there was a nation until that time; and at that time your people, everyone who is found written in the book, will be rescued" (**NASB**).

- Satan on earth

Jude 9 - "But Michael the archangel, when he disputed with the devil and argued about the body of Moses, did not dare pronounce against him a railing judgment, but said, 'The Lord rebuke you!'" (**NASB**).

- Satan in heaven

Revelation 12:7 - "And there was war in heaven, Michael and his angels waging war with the dragon. The dragon and his angels waged war" (**NASB**).

THE "FALLEN" ARCHANGEL "SON of the MORNING" / LUCIFER / SATAN

Lucifer is thought to be the original name for the devil. This name does not reflect the present character of Satan but rather his original created purpose and character. Lucifer originally possessed a high place in heaven:

Isaiah 14:12 - "How you have fallen from heaven, morning star, son of the dawn! You have been cast down to the earth, you who once laid low the nations" (**NIV**)!

Perhaps the highest above all angels, but was cast down because of his desire to rise above God.

The name Lucifer means bearer of light, reflecting his purpose to bear the light of God. By bearing light, angels are messengers of God. Hence, Lucifer should have been a light bearer to Jesus himself who is the true Light, which lighteth every man that cometh into the world:

John 1:9 - "The true light that gives light to everyone was coming into the world" **(NIV)**.

Satan is the adversary of God and mankind. He is the fallen angel, the devil, who rebelled against God. He's mentioned many times in the New Testament:

Matthew 4:10 - "Then Jesus said to him, 'Go, Satan! For it is written, You shall worship the Lord your God, and serve Him only.'" **(NASB)**.

Mark 1:13 - "And He was in the wilderness forty days being tempted by Satan; and He was with the wild beasts, and the angels were ministering to Him" **(NASB)**.

Luke 22:3 - "And Satan entered into Judas who was called Iscariot, belonging to the number of the twelve" **(NASB)**.

Romans 16:20 - "The God of peace will soon crush Satan under your feet. The grace of our Lord Jesus be with you" **(NASB)**.

II Corinthians 11:14 - "No wonder, for even Satan disguises himself as an angel of light" **(NASB)**.

Revelations 12:9 - "And the great dragon was thrown down, the serpent of old who is called the devil and Satan, who deceives the whole world; he was thrown down to the earth, and his angels were thrown down with him" **(NASB)**.

The other opinion which says that the expression the "Angel of the Lord" is not really an Angel, or Michael, but the Word of God, God Himself, is regarded presently as a mere speculation and obsolete opinion (Oehler, 1983). As long as God's children are exposed to the attacks of Satan in this world, Michael's battle cry: "Who is like God?" will continue to terrify, shatter and defeat all the forces of evil. A verse of scripture comes to mind: (Parente, 1994).

> **Matthew 16:18** - "And I say also unto thee, that thou art Peter, and upon this rock I will build my church; and the gates of hell shall not prevail against it" **(KJV)**.

The Church Will Never Fail!

Names of Angels

Angels Walk Among Us

CHAPTER 5
Fallen Angels or Demons

God created Satan as one of Heaven's most beautiful angels. Lucifer means "light-bearer" and was referred to as the "morning star." However, the devil was jealous and rebelled against God. The devil's prideful revolt and greed for power turned him into a self-proclaimed enemy of God. He wanted to replace God in every way. Regardless of what name he is called, he is not on an equal plain with God. A careful reading of Scripture helps us understand why Lucifer fell from heaven. He was created perfectly; however, inner iniquity and violence led him to sin. Isaiah describes what happened in Lucifer's heart when he decided it was no longer good enough to be a perfect angel created in the beauty of God. Notice the five "I will" statements of Lucifer found in Isaiah:

> **Isaiah 14:12-15** - "How you are fallen from heaven, O Lucifer, son of the morning! How are you cut down to the ground, you who weakened the nations! For you have said in your heart: '**I will** ascend into heaven, **I will** exalt my throne above the stars of God; **I will** also sit on the mount of the congregation on the farthest sides of the north; **I will** ascend above the heights of the clouds, **I will** be like the Most High.' Yet you shall be brought down to Sheol, to the lowest depths of the Pit" **(KJV)**.

Fallen angels are created spiritual beings who rebelled against God. Fallen angels are those angels who rebelled against God along with Lucifer, an archangel who became the devil. Most scholars agree that one-third of the angels fell into sin and became demons. Following are verses often quoted in reference to the evil one:

> **Revelation 12:3-4** - "And there appeared another wonder in heaven; and behold a great red dragon, having seven heads and ten horns, and seven crowns upon his heads. And his tail drew the third part of the stars of heaven, and did cast them to the earth: and the dragon stood before the woman which was ready to be delivered, for to devour her child as soon as it was born" **(KJV)**.

In the future, there will be a judgment upon the fallen angels:

> **Matthew 25:41** - "Then shall he say also unto them on the left hand, Depart from me, ye cursed, into everlasting fire, prepared for the devil and his angels" **(KJV)**.
>
> **II Peter 2:4** - "For if God spared not the angels that sinned, but cast them down to hell, and delivered them into chains of darkness, to be reserved unto judgment;" **(KJV)**.
>
> **Jude 6** - "And the angels which kept not their first estate, but left their own habitation, he hath reserved in everlasting chains under darkness unto the judgment of the great day" **(KJV)**.
>
> **Revelation 12:9** - "And the great dragon was cast out, that old serpent, called the Devil, and Satan, who deceives the whole world: he was cast out into the earth, and his angels were cast out with him" **(KJV)**.

Demons are mentioned in nineteen out of the twenty-seven New Testament books, and Jesus frequently claimed to "cast out demons":

> **Matthew 12:27** - "And if I by Beelzebub cast out devils, by whom do your children cast them out? therefore they shall be your judges" **(KJV)**.

We know that hell was prepared for the devil and his angels, according to:

> **Matthew 25:41** - "Then He will also say to those on His left, 'Depart from Me, accursed ones, into the eternal fire which has been prepared for the devil and his angels'" **(NASB)**.

Jesus, by using the possessive word his makes it clear that these angels belong to Satan:

> **Revelation 12:7-9** - "And there was war in heaven, Michael and his angels waging war with the dragon. The dragon and his angels waged war, and they were not strong enough, and there was no longer a place found for them in heaven. And the great dragon was thrown down, the serpent of old who is called the devil and Satan, who deceives the whole world; he was thrown down to the earth, and his angels were thrown down with him" **(NASB)**.

What is the purpose of demons? Just as God's angels are sent to praise Him and aid believers, Satan and his demons are bent on the desecrating God's name in the earth and the destruction and deception of all those who love and serve Him:

> **I Peter 5:8** - "Be of sober *spirit*, be on the alert. Your adversary, the devil, prowls around like a roaring lion, seeking someone to devour" **(NASB)**.

II Corinthians 4:4 - "In whose case the god of this [a]world has blinded the minds of the unbelieving so that they might not see the light of the gospel of the glory of Christ, who is the image of God" **(NASB)**.

II Corinthians 11:14-15 - "No wonder, for even Satan disguises himself as an angel of light. Therefore it is not surprising if his servants also disguise themselves as servants of righteousness, whose end will be according to their deeds" **(NASB)**.

The Bible calls demons "evil spirits" and "unclean":

Matthew 10:1 - "Jesus summoned His twelve disciples and gave them authority over unclean spirits, to cast them out, and to heal every kind of disease and every kind of sickness" **(NASB)**.

Immediately. the news about Him spread everywhere into all the surrounding district of Galilee.

Mark 1:27 - "They were all amazed, so that they debated among themselves, saying, "What is this? A new teaching with authority! He commands even the unclean spirits, and they obey Him" **(NASB)**.

And this passage asserts that they are indeed the angels of Satan:

Revelation 12:9 - "The great dragon was hurled down—that ancient serpent called the devil, or Satan, who leads the whole world astray. He was hurled to the earth, and his angels with him" **(NIV)**.

Satan and his demons also attack Christians:

II Corinthians 12:7 - "Or because of these surpassingly great revelations. Therefore, in order to keep me from becoming conceited, I was given a thorn in my flesh, a messenger of Satan, to torment me" **(NIV)**.

And do battle with the holy angels:

Revelation 12:4-9 - "Its tail swept a third of the stars out of the sky and flung them to the earth. The dragon stood in front of the woman who was about to give birth, so that it might devour her child the moment he was born. She gave birth to a son, a male child, who "will rule all the nations with an iron scepter." And her child was snatched up to God and to his throne. The woman fled into the wilderness to a place prepared for her by God, where she might be taken care of for 1,260 days. Then war broke out in heaven. Michael and his angels fought against the dragon, and the dragon and his angels fought back. But he was not strong enough, and they lost their place in heaven. The great dragon was hurled down—that ancient serpent called the devil, or Satan, who leads the whole world astray. He was hurled to the earth, and his angels with him" **(NIV)**.

Fallen angels in the Bible are often referred to as the "sons of God" and as Satan's ministers.

Satan, with his army of fallen angels and demons, are determined to corrupt and destroy all that is good and godly. But God gives us authority over the evil of this enemy as Jesus tells us in:

Luke 10: 19-20 - "I have given you authority to trample on snakes and scorpions and to overcome all the power of the enemy; nothing will harm you. However, do not rejoice that the spirits submit to you, but rejoice that your names are written in heaven" **(NIV)**.

The following is a short list of the capabilities of fallen angels:

1. Physical Visibility:

Although fallen angels are spiritual beings, they appear to have the ability to physically appear to people, like their unfallen counterparts:

> **Genesis 19:1** - "And there came two angels to Sodom at even; and Lot sat in the gate of Sodom: and Lot seeing them rose up to meet them; and he bowed himself with his face toward the ground;" **(KJV)**.

2. Extraterrestrial Travel:

Fallen Angels apparently can travel out of this world. For instance, Satan and his fallen angels one day came to present themselves in front of God in Heaven:

> **Job 1:6** - "Now there was a day when the sons of God came to present themselves before the LORD, and Satan came also among them" **(KJV)**.

3. Physical Transformation and the Ability to Deceive:

II Corinthians 11 informs us that Satan's ministers and fallen angels have the ability to transform themselves so that they can pose as ministers of righteousness:

> **II Corinthians 11:13-15** - "For such ones are false apostles, deceitful workers transforming themselves into apostles of Christ. And did not Satan marvelously transform himself into an angel of light? It is not a great thing, then, if also his ministers transform themselves as ministers of righteousness, whose end will be according to their works" **(KJV)**.

Therefore, fallen angels have the ability to deceive people by transforming themselves to resemble religious figures that many people believe in if they choose to do that which they sometimes actually do.

Here are a few abilities of demons:

- ***The Ability to Control the Entity they Possess:***

A well-known event where Christ cast out demons from a man to a herd of swine suggest demons can control the entity they possess. The demons controlled the man's actions and then the actions of the herd of swine.

> **Matthew 8:28-32** - "And when he was come to the other side into the country of the Gergesenes, there met him two possessed with devils, coming out of the tombs, exceeding fierce, so that no man might pass by that way. And, behold, they cried out, saying, What have we to do with thee, Jesus, thou Son of God? art thou come hither to torment us before the time? And there was a good way off from them an herd of many swine feeding. So the devils besought him, saying, If thou cast us out, suffer us to go away into the herd of swine. And he said unto them, Go. And when they were come out, they went into the herd of swine: and, behold, the whole herd of swine ran violently down a steep place into the sea, and perished in the waters" **(KJV)**.

> **Mark 5:11-13** - "Now there was there nigh unto the mountains a great herd of swine feeding. And all the devils besought him, saying, Send us into the swine, that we may enter into them. And forthwith Jesus

gave them leave. And the unclean spirits went out, and entered into the swine: and the herd ran violently down a steep place into the sea, (they were about two thousand;) and were choked in the sea" **(KJV)**.

- ***Ability to Inflict Harm on their Victim(s):***

Matthew 4 and **Luke 4** suggest that demons have the power to inflict mental illness and physical diseases on their victims:

Matthew 4:23-25 - "And Jesus went about all Galilee, teaching in their synagogues, and preaching the gospel of the kingdom, and healing all manner of sickness and all manner of disease among the people. And his fame went throughout all Syria: and they brought unto him all sick people that were taken with divers diseases and torments, and those which were possessed with devils, and those which were lunatick, and those that had the palsy; and he healed them. And there followed him great multitudes of people from Galilee, and from Decapolis, and from Jerusalem, and from Judaea, and from beyond Jordan" **(KJV)**.

Luke 4:40-41 - "Now when the sun was setting, all they that had any sick with divers diseases brought them unto him; and he laid his hands on every one of them, and healed them. And devils also came out of many, crying out, and saying, Thou art Christ the Son of God. And he rebuking them suffered them not to speak: for they knew that he was Christ" **(KJV)**.

- ***Unusual Physical Strength:***

The episode when Christ cast out demons into swine also suggests that demons can give an individual they possess unusual strength:

Mark 5:1-5 - "And they came over unto the other side of the sea, into the country of the Gadarenes. And when he was come out of the ship, immediately there met him out of the tombs a man with an unclean spirit, Who had his dwelling among the tombs; and no man could bind him, no, not with chains: Because that he had been often bound with fetters and chains, and the chains had been plucked asunder by him, and the fetters broken in pieces: neither could any man tame him. And always, night and day, he was in the mountains, and in the tombs, crying, and cutting himself with stones" **(KJV)**.

You may be wondering how could a perfect, holy being fall? How could the first unholy affection arise his angelic being? Lucifer was created by God with one attribute exactly like you and I have; he had freedom to choose. Lucifer could have chosen humble obedience; instead, he chose prideful rebellion (Outlaw, 2019).

While the description of demons/fallen angels and their efforts may sound scary, remember they are defeated enemies of God. **Colossians 2:15** tells us that Christ has "disarmed the powers and authorities" and He has "made a public spectacle of them, triumphing over them by the cross." God's love conquered sin and death, triumphing over Satan and all his empty promises. While we are surrounded by a host of angels and demons engaged in battles and victories, God uses his angels to accomplish his goal of protecting us from the enemy and his evil ways. We are protected from the Evil One, and the forces of evil active around us in the world today. Thankfully, we are warned of these forces in the Bible. It is our responsibility to recognize them, and when we notice the presence of evil, respond accordingly (White, 2013).

We are not to fear demons because God offers us the equipment to resist the devil and his demons.

> **James 4:7** - "Submit yourselves, then, to God. Resist the devil, and he will flee from you" **(NIV)**.

Paul explains that we can win:

> **Ephesians 6:11-12** - "Put on the full armor of God so that you can take your stand against the devil's schemes. For our struggle is not against flesh and blood, but against the rulers, against the authorities, against the powers of this dark world and against the spiritual forces of evil in the heavenly realms" **(NIV)**.

> **I John 3:8** - "The one who does what is sinful is of the devil, because the devil has been sinning from the beginning. The reason the Son of God appeared was to destroy the devil's work" **(NIV)**.

Another major difference is how angels and demons show up in human form. Warner Wallace, author of Cold-Case Christianity says "Angels Appear Human/Demons Inhabit Humans". While angels and demons aren't always in human form, they can show up this way. However, their objectives are very different. Angels appear in human form to show their empathy and love for us. Demons will enter the human body to take on the form of those they are attacking. Jesus encountered many demons during His earthly ministry (2018):

> **Matthew 8:16** tells us, "When evening came, many who were demon-possessed were brought to Jesus, and he drove out the spirits with a word and healed all the sick" **(NIV)**.

Jesus was able to drive out the spirits with one word. The Bible also tells us that demons were afraid of Jesus.

Matthew 8:29 tells us that the demons asked Jesus "'What do you want with us, Son of God?' They shouted. 'Have you come here to torture us before the appointed time'" **(NIV)**?

Those demons knew who Jesus was and knew their end would be of torment. They recognized His power and shuddered in His presence (Wallace, 2013).

Angels and demons are very real, active, and about the work of their masters. But the difference is whom they work for. Angels are created beings, created by God for the purpose of serving Him. Demons used to be God's angels but rebelled against him and were kicked out of heaven with Satan. Now, they work to do evil with him as their master. Jesus says of Satan and his demons:

John 10:10 - "The thief comes only to steal and kill and destroy; I have come that they may have life, and have it to the full" **(NIV)**.

Satan is also known as a tempter, oppressor, and deceiver.

John 8:44 - "Ye are of your father the devil, and the lusts of your father ye will do. He was a murderer from the beginning, and abode not in the truth, because there is no truth in him. When he speaketh a lie, he speaketh of his own: for he is a liar, and the father of it" **(KJV)**.

His minions are sent about to undermine all good, love, and righteousness of God. Satan and his demons are in a spiritual battle with God's angels for control and over the eternal destiny of human souls.

Psalms 68:17 - "The chariots of God are tens of thousands and thousands of thousands; the Lord has come from Sinai into his sanctuary" **(NIV)**.

Psalm 91:11 - "For he will command his angels concerning you to guard you in all your ways" **(NIV)**.

Satan, with his army of fallen angels and demons, are determined to corrupt and destroy all that is good and godly. We are warned in:

I Peter 5:8 - "Be self-controlled and alert. Your enemy the devil prowls around like a roaring lion looking for someone to devour" **(NIV)**.

God gives us authority over the evil of this enemy as Jesus tells us in:

Luke 10:19-20 - "I have given you authority to trample on snakes and scorpions and to overcome all the power of the enemy; nothing will harm you. However, do not rejoice that the spirits submit to you, but rejoice that your names are written in heaven" **(NIV)**.

All created beings have two choices, to accept this authority over the evil enemy or to follow Satan into:

Matthew 25:41 - "Then shall he say also unto them on the left hand, Depart from me, ye cursed, into everlasting fire, prepared for the devil and his angels" **(KJV)**.

The Bible also teaches that angels are not exempt from judgment. Paul asked the Corinthians:

I Corinthians 6:3 - "Do you not know that we are to judge angels" **(NIV)**?

Toward the end of the age, it will be our responsibility as Christians to represent God in the role of judge. It may be that during the Tribulation, the millennial kingdom, or eternity to follow. We will serve as judges similar to the judges who ruled before Israel's first king. As judges, we will be given a position of authority over angels.

God's angels serve believers as ministering spirits as they did with Jesus Christ in:

Matthew 4:11 - "Then the devil left Him; and behold, angels came and *began* to minister to Him" (**NASB**).

They are used as messengers of God and mighty warriors throughout the Bible. As mighty and comforting as God's angels are, they are His servants and not to be glorified above Him. Oxford Professor and author C.S. Lewis said, "There are two equal and opposite errors into which our race can fall into about devils. One is to disbelieve in their existence. The other is to believe, and to have an excessive and unhealthy interest in them" (Outlaw, 2019).

Fallen Angels or Demons

Angels Walk Among Us

CHAPTER 6
Encounters with Angels

Since the beginning of time, God has sent celestial beings to help people on earth. We are not alone! When we pray, "Thy kingdom come, Thy will be done on earth as it is in heaven," we are welcoming heaven's hosts to come join us, aid us, and strengthen us. They're ready to come. God's Word emphasizes great spiritual activity in the latter-days. Jesus Himself said, "The end-of-the-age is the harvest," and promised to send an angelic host to co-labor with us in the mandate to see Him receive the full measure of His reward. There will be a harvest of promises, commissions, mantles, and a harvest of souls.

Many people have reported experiences of some type of help that seemed to involve angels. Some are quite overt; others are more subtle. Of course, not all stories are genuine nor are they recalled accurately. Nevertheless, there are many other stories that really happened as reported.

People from all over the world have reported encounters with mysterious beings. They appear to bring important messages or lend much-needed assistance, then vanish without a trace. Could they be angels or even guardian angels? Some of the most fascinating and uplifting stories of the unexplained are those that people perceive as being miraculous in nature. Sometimes they take the form of answered prayer or are interpreted as the actions of guardian angels. These remarkable events and encounters lend comfort, strengthen faith, and even save lives. They almost always seem to happen when they are needed most. Are they literally from heaven, or are they the result of the interaction of our consciousness with a profoundly mysterious universe? However, you view them, these real-life experiences are worth our attention (Godwin, 1990).

Do We Have a Guardian Angel?

An old tradition says that guardian angels are appointed to children at the time of their birth. The seventeenth-century mystic Amos Komensky declared that each child had an angel "given to him by God and ordained to be his guardian, that the angel might guard him, preserve him, and protect him against all dangers and snares, pits, ambushes, traps, and temptations" (Encyclopedia of the Unusual and Unexplained, 2003).

Although the Holy Bible never uses the term "guardian angel," one of the most treasured beliefs still held by many people is that each person has an appointed guardian angel to watch over them (Outlaw, 2016):

- *There are examples of angels being assigned to protect human beings:*

Acts 12:6-10 - "On the very night when Herod was about to bring him forward, Peter was sleeping between two soldiers, bound with two chains, and guards in front of the door were watching over the prison. And behold, an angel of the Lord suddenly appeared, and a light shone in the cell; and he struck Peter's side and woke him up, saying, 'Get up quickly.' And his chains fell off his hands. And the angel said to him, 'Gird yourself and put on your sandals.' And he did so. And he said to him, 'Wrap your cloak around you and follow me.' And he went out and continued to follow, and he did not know that what was being done by the angel was real, but thought he saw a vision. When they had passed the first and second guard, they came to the iron gate that leads into the city, which opened for them by itself; and they went out and went along one street, and immediately the angel departed from him" **(NASB)**.

- *Angels are celestial messengers that move at the speed of light to carry out God's will:*

Ezekiel 1:14 - "And the living beings ran to and fro like bolts of lightning" **(NASB)**.

- *In times of peril, "guardian" angels are God's servants sent to rescue us:*

II Kings 6:13-17 - "So he said, 'Go and see where he is, that I may send and take him.' And it was told him, saying, 'Behold, he is in Dothan.' He sent horses and chariots and a great army there, and they came by night and surrounded the city. Now when the attendant of the man of God had risen early and gone out, behold, an army with horses and chariots was circling the city. And his servant said to him, 'Alas, my master! What shall we do?' So he answered, 'Do not fear, for those who are with us are more than those who are with them.' Then Elisha prayed and said, 'O

LORD, I pray, open his eyes that he may see.' And the LORD opened the servant's eyes, and he saw; and behold, the mountain was full of horses and chariots of fire all around Elisha" (**NASB**).

- *Angels involve themselves in the political affairs of nations as well as the smallest concerns of children.*

Isaiah 37:33-36 - "Therefore thus saith the LORD concerning the king of Assyria, He shall not come into this city, nor shoot an arrow there, nor come before it with shields, nor cast a bank against it. By the way that he came, by the same shall he return, and shall not come into this city, saith the LORD. For I will defend this city to save it for own mine sake, and for my servant David's sake. Then the angel of the LORD went forth, and smote in the camp of the Assyrians a hundred and fourscore and five thousand and when they arose early in the morning, behold, they were all dead corpses" (**KJV**).

Matthew 18:10 - "Take heed that ye despise not one of these little ones; for I say unto you, That in heaven their angels do always behold the face of my Father which is in heaven" (**NASB**).

- *Angels Excel in Strength*

Matthew 28:2 - "There was a violent earthquake, for an angel of the Lord came down from heaven and going to the tomb, rolled back the stone and sat on it" (**NIV**).

- *Angels are Spirits*

Hebrews 1:7 - "In speaking of the angels he says, 'He makes his angels spirits and his servants flames of fire'" (**NIV**).

Hebrews 1:14 - "Are not all angels ministering spirits sent to serve those who will inherit salvation" **(NIV)**?

- *Angels are Bright*

Matthew 28:2-4 - "And, behold, there was a great earthquake: for the angel of the Lord descended from heaven, and came and rolled back the stone from the door, and sat upon it. His countenance was like lightning, and his raiment white as snow: And for fear of him the keepers did shake, and became as dead men" **(KJV)**.

- *Angels are Wise*

Angels have wisdom and intelligence. They are smarter than we are, but they are not omniscient (all-knowing).

Hebrews 2:7 - "Thou maddest him a little lower than the angels; thou crownedst him with glory and honour, and didst set him over the works of thy hands" **(KJV)**.

- *Angels are Ministers*

Angels can act as ministers to those in need.

I Kings 19:5 - "Then he lay down under the bush and fell asleep. All at once an angel touched him and said, 'Get up and eat'" **(NIV)**.

I Kings 19:7 - "The angel of the LORD came back a second time and touched him and said, 'Get up and eat, for the journey is too much for you'" **(NIV)**.

Matthew 4:11 - "Then the devil left him, and angels came and attended Him" **(NIV)**.

Luke 22:43 - "An angel from heaven appeared to him and strengthened Him" **(NIV)**.

Hebrews 1:14 - "Are not all angels ministering spirits sent to serve those who will inherit salvation" **(NIV)**?

In his book, *Angels: God's Secret Agents,* Billy Graham states, "I do not believe in angels because I have ever seen one, because I haven't. I believe in angels because the Bible says there are angels; I believe the Bible to be the true Word of God" (1975). Angels serve in an anonymous manner that assures all glory goes to God. How else would we explain the bright aura that rescued two young boys from a collapsing cavern or the tall blond stranger that guided the divers to a hole in the ice? A young boy rolls, unharmed, across three lanes of California freeway and asks, "Mother, did you see them? All the angels that stopped the traffic?" Angels never minister selfishly nor do they direct attention to themselves (Guidepost, 1993).

I Peter 3:22 - "Who is gone into heaven and is on the right hand of God; angels and authorities and powers being made subject unto him" **(KJV)**.

Most comforting are David's words of the protective care angels provide to God's children.

Psalms 91:9-13 - "Because you have made the Lord, who is my refuge, even the Most High, your dwelling place, no evil shall befall you, nor shall any plague come near your dwelling; for He shall give His angels charge over you, to keep you in all your ways. In their hands, they shall bear you up, lest you dash your foot against a stone. You shall tread upon the lion and the cobra, the young lion and the serpent you shall trample underfoot" **(RSV)**.

A brief reference made by Jesus about angels shows how each one of us has at least one of these celestial guardians of heaven watching over us. Jesus Christ said:

> **Matthew 18:10** - "Take heed that you do not despise one of these little ones, for I say to you that in heaven their angels always see the face of My Father who is in heaven" **(NIV)**.

God created angels for many purposes, to include guiding, protecting, encouraging and strengthening children of God. We are taught in scripture that angels are God's servants, sent by Him into the world to serve His will. There is a description in the Bible of millions of angels praising God in Heaven, so perhaps a primary role of angels is to praise and glorify God. God has also commanded His angels concerning you. We may not see them but we should know that angels are watching over us to transport blessings into our lives, to deliver messages of hope and encouragement, to protect us from danger and to help us glorify God. Scripture proves it (White, 2013).

> **Psalm 91:11-12** - "For he will command his angels concerning you to guard you in all your ways; they will lift you up in their hands, so that you will not strike your foot against a stone" **(NIV)**.

God offers not only protection and guidance through the use of His angels, but also his pure and selfless love. According to the psalmist, God can command one or more angels to guard and defend us in our circumstances.

> **Exodus 23:20** states "See, I am sending an angel ahead of you to guard you along the way and to bring you to the place I have prepared" **(NIV)**.

It is here that the Lord promises the Israelites that they would be guided and guarded in their way through the wilderness to the Promised Land of Canaan. This was no ordinary angel. This was the Angel of the Lord, an Old Testament manifestation of Christ Himself. In **Exodus 23:21**, the Lord declares, "... My Name Is In Him." This promise was connected with the rule that the Israelites must be obedient to the angel God sent before them. Michael is also listed as the guardian prince of Israel:

> **Daniel 12:1** - "At that time Michael, the great prince who protects your people, will arise. There will be a time of distress such as has not happened from the beginning of nations until then. But at that time your people, everyone whose name is found written in the book, will be delivered" **(NIV)**.

There is no doubt that God's angels help protect us. They also reveal information and minister to believers in general. The big question for many people is whether each person is assigned a guardian angel. While Scripture does not state that a specific angel is assigned to every individual, we know that we are in the presence of angels, and they are here for good:

> **Hebrews 1:14** states "Are not all angels ministering spirits sent to serve those who will inherit salvation" **(NIV)**?

Angels are sent by God to protect us and minister to us and to carry out His will and work for good in our lives. We know from this verse from Hebrews that angels are sent to serve those who are going to receive salvation. By definition, salvation is deliverance from sin, brought about by faith in Jesus Christ.

> **Hebrews 13:2** - "Do not forget to show hospitality to strangers, for by so doing some people have shown hospitality to angels without knowing it" **(NIV)**.

We are called in this verse to be hospitable or friendly to those we don't know. The Bible tells us that we may be talking with or hosting messengers of God, unaware. When we meet strangers, we should be careful how we treat them because it could be one of God's angels sent by God to help us or protect us. We don't know what God is trying to do or what He is trying to accomplish, but we know that it is a part of His good and perfect will.

Worshipping or giving honor to angels is idolatry:

Colossians 2:18 - "Do not let anyone who delights in false humility and the worship of angels disqualify you. Such a person also goes into great detail about what they have seen; they are puffed up with idle notions by their nonspiritual mind" **(NIV)**.

We are warned about the danger of pursuing angels instead of God because Paul says in:

II Corinthians 11:14 - "And no wonder, for Satan himself masquerades as an angel of light" **(NIV)**.

We must not place our faith in angels, which God created. Let us put our faith in God who rules and commands the angels. It is God who continues to do extraordinary feats in our lives, dispatching His angelic hosts on our behalf (Outlaw, 2015).

Stories & Testimonies

Interest in angels is higher than it has ever been!

Poll findings in the American magazine, *The Skeptic*, reflect that seven out of ten people believe in angels, and one in three have witnessed the presence of a celestial being. *The Skeptic* also reported that the highest growth in the area of beliefs is in angels (Fry, 1999).

Emma Heathcote, a graduate of theology from Birmingham University, UK, is researching angel encounters. Gill Fry interviewed her for *Share International*. Heathcote found that angels are mentioned in all religions and they always seem to play similar roles to everyone (Fry, 1999).

For many people who have written to me, their angelic experience has given them hope, calm and reassurance, and for others, and has often helped them out of a difficult or dangerous situation. I heard from one man who was waiting to cross a busy road on his way to work. Seeing a gap in the traffic, he stepped out, only for an elderly lady he'd never seen before to stretch her arm out in front of his chest with such force it prevented him from crossing. Seconds later a sports car sped pasted which would otherwise certainly have hit him. He turned around to thank the woman, but she was nowhere to be seen. In that kind of life-threatening situation the angel often then disappears (Fry, 1999).

All of these many different experiences can be categorized as follows: (1) Strength to cope with and accept terminal illness, (2) Bedroom visitations, (3) Helping out in a practical hour of need, (4) Prevention of fatal accident, (5) Companionship when afraid, (6) Help to reassess life and see things from a different angle, (7) Guardian angels, (8) Angel experiences around a church, (9) No reasonable explanation for the experience, and (10) Those who see angels all the time.

Heathcote found that when there are angelic visitations, they seem to fall into five main categories:

1. *The first is visual*, where the angel appears in either traditional winged-angel or human form, often as a figure in white.

2. *The second experience is an unexplained strong, sweet scent*, which is very common at the time of death.

3. *A third category is hearing a voice or a choir of angels*, often inside a place of worship.

4. *A fourth category is an actual physical feeling*, which often happens to elderly people. The sense of wings being enveloped around them is a common occurrence. One elderly woman wrote to me and described how, when her husband died, she hated going to bed because she missed him so much, and explained how she would see and feel her duvet turn into a pair of angelic wing-like,comforting arms. Interestingly, she was an atheist. I've heard from several people who, at a time of needing comfort, experienced wings enveloping them but there was no visible angel. Another kind of physical feeling is touch. One woman wrote to me relating how, at her son's funeral, she saw an angel and felt it touch her cheek. Countless people who have written to me have not only seen but have felt the touch of an angel.

5. *The fifth category is light*: either a beam or a ray of light. Often at the time of a loved one's death, a flash of light seems to shoot upwards. One writer described seeing her father slip from the bottom of the bed, stand next to an angel, look around the room and then pass upwards into the beam of light. The mother was also in the room, and although she didn't see this, she sensed what was happening. Many experiences occur around death, hence the expression of the angel of death (Fry, 1999).

One man wrote to me about an incident in the hospital when his wife was seriously ill on a ventilator in the intensive care ward. He was visiting her with his two sons and his parents. Her condition became critical; she had a 50-50 chance of survival. Suddenly her husband saw an angel standing at the end of the bed behind the metal bars. While he wondered whether this was merely the result of being stressed and upset, his son turned to him and asked: "Dad, can you see that figure behind the bed?" The younger son then replied: "It's an angel!" and his parents exclaimed that they "had never seen anything like it." When a nurse came over, they asked her if she could see anything unusual, and she replied: "Oh my goodness, there is an angel!" The angel then disappeared, and from that moment the woman made a full recovery (Fry, 1999).

There was another case in a small parish church near London. A young couple had moved to the area, and the wife asked to be confirmed. She was at the font waiting to be confirmed, and the vicar felt a strange sensation of warm oil all over his body. He noticed all the congregation were looking intently at the woman and when he turned, an angel was standing next to her with its hand on her shoulder. One witness fainted but all the people near the front of the church saw the angel. The vicar gathered these people together the next day and found that they had all had the same experience (Fry, 1999).

I have heard from many people aged between 20 and 40 about experiences they had as children. The first letter I received was from a Justice of the Peace in her 60's relating an experience that happened when she was 22 years old. She was working in the casualty department at Guy's Hospital in London. A three-year-old girl was rushed into casualty followed by her hysterical mother, a policeman, a witness, and a distraught juggernaut driver. Apparently, the child had been playing in the road when a force had driven over her. The driver felt the wheels go over her and was extremely distressed. All four people had seen the accident. The doctor examined the child, and there was nothing wrong. X-rays were taken, and everything was normal except that she was unconscious. Eventually, she came round, looked up to her mother and said: "Where's the man in the long white coat?" The doctor stepped forward, but the child said: "No, there is a man in a long white coat and he picked me up when the wheels went over" (Fry, 1999).

> **Revelation 5:11-12** - "Then I looked and heard the voice of many angels, numbering thousands upon thousands, and ten thousand times ten thousand. They encircled the throne and the living creatures and the elders. In a loud voice, they sang: 'Worthy is the Lamb, who was slain, to receive power and wealth and wisdom and strength and honor and glory and praise'" **(NIV)**.

Try to envision millions of angels encircling God's throne and glorifying the Lord. We see a different side here of these fascinating and beautiful spiritual beings. Not only do they serve a role as God's messengers and as our guardians, but they also praise God and serve as His warriors. You can rest assured that you are being cared for at this very moment by God's angels. What a wonderful creator God is!

> **Psalm 103:19-22** - "The LORD has established His throne in heaven, and His kingdom rules over all. Praise the LORD, you His angels, you mighty ones who do His bidding, who obey His word. Praise the LORD, all His heavenly hosts, you His servants who do His will. Praise the LORD, all His works everywhere in His dominion. Praise the LORD, my soul" **(NIV)**.

Having celebrated God's mercy to His people, the psalmist praises God's excellent majesty and universal dominion. The psalmist also acknowledges God's angels, who do His bidding, intervene and protect on His behalf, and are obedient to His will. God commands those faithful spirits who are nearest to Him, who come from Him and are marked by Him to defend us in all our ways.

AMEN!

Encounters with Angels

Angels Walk Among Us

CHAPTER 7
Gathering of the Angels

Angels appear in the Bible from the beginning to the end, from the Book of Genesis to the Book of Revelation. The Bible is our best source of knowledge about angels and teaches that God created them. He sends His angels to deliver messages to us and to help guide, guard, and direct our lives. Angels have been present at most major events in Bible history. Hopefully, at the conclusion of this chapter, you will know more about angels and why they are here. Angels are purely spiritual beings that do God's will:

> **Psalms 103:20** - "Bless the LORD, ye his angels, that excel in strength, that do His commandments, hearkening unto the voice of his word" **(KJV)**.
>
> **Matthew 26:53** - "Thinkest thou that I cannot now pray to my Father, and He shall presently give me more than twelve legions of angels" **(KJV)**?

Angels worship God as we do, but they worship and praise Him continually and never stop. In Revelation it says:

> **Revelation 4:8** - "Each of the four living creatures had six wings and was covered with eyes all around, even under his wings. Day and night they never stop saying: 'Holy, holy, holy is the Lord God Almighty, who was, and is, and is to come'" **(NIV)**.

Like us angels don't know everything God knows. The Bible says that not even the angels know when he is going to come and take us to heaven:

> **Matthew 24:36** - "But about that day or hour no one knows, not even the angels in heaven, nor the Son, but only the Father" **(NIV)**.

Angels are also different from us in some ways, too. They live in heaven with God so they certainly know more about God than we do, and just being in God's presence may give them the special glow or brightness they seem to display. Angels can be visible on some missions and invisible during other tasks. They were seen at Jesus' tomb and seen in the sky to the shepherds, but they can be invisible when they come to our aide and we may never know that they are there. A very distinctive difference between God's angels and us: The Bible tells us that angels never die.

> **Luke 20:36** - "And they can no longer die; for they are like the angels. They are God's children, since they are children of the resurrection" **(NIV)**.

So you can see that angels are higher than us in the hierarchy of God's creations, but always lower than their creator. God is very clear in saying that we should not worship angels or see them as more important than Him. He is the only one we should pray to, but we can certainly be thankful to Him for angels and for the missions of compassion He directs them to accomplish on our behalf.

You might wonder what angels look like. Well, there is no clear answer to this. When people saw angels in Biblical times, we are told they were often afraid at first sight. Most of us would probably have the same response today if an angel were to appear suddenly in front of us. I think its safe to think of angels as friendly, beautiful, spiritual creations that help us as God wills.

Angels have been mentioned in different groupings. Some are called "chief princes", "cherubim" or "seraphims". They all seem to be important to God and all seem to have specific duties that they perform. While there obviously are many things about angels that we do not know, it is clear that these rational, spiritual beings serve a useful place in the divine scheme of things. It is further apparent that much of the folklore being popularized these days by the entertainment media has no basis in reality (Jackson, 2019).

Angels apparently experience some joy. One of the more unique things about angels is that whenever a person becomes a Christian and accepts Christ as their Savior, they sing and rejoice.

> **Luke 15:10** - "In the same way, I tell you, there is rejoicing in the presence of the angels of God over one sinner who repents" **(NIV)**.

One day we can look forward to singing to God with the angels. These celestial beings are very real creations of God and will accompany the Lord when He returns:

> **Matthew 25:31-32** - "When the Son of Man comes in His glory, and all the holy angels with Him, then He will sit on the throne of His glory: All the nations will be gathered before Him, and He will separate them one from another, as a shepherd divides his sheep from the goats" **(KJV)**.

It is important that we note the number of times that God used angels to carry out his will. I started in the Old Testament showing examples and then showed the times and events where God sent angels to do his bidding in the New testament.

OLD TESTAMENT

- *Present at Creation*

When God created the world, it seems it was witnessed by angels.

> **Job 38:4** - "Where wast thou when I laid the foundations of the earth? declare, if thou hast understanding" (**KJV**).

> **Job 38:7** - "When the morning stars sang together, and all the sons of God shouted for joy" (**KJV**)?

- *Fall of Adam*

God positioned cherubims to protect the Garden of Eden after the fall of Adam and Eve in:

> **Genesis 3:24** - "So he drove out the man; and he placed at the east of the garden of Eden Cherubims, and a flaming sword which turned every way, to keep the way of the tree of life" (**KJV**).

- *Hagar*

Although angels were likely present at creation, there is no mention of their ministry until the days of Abraham. After Hagar had conceived Abraham's child, she was sent out by Sarah, Abraham's wife. The angel of the LORD found Hagar.

> **Genesis 16:7** - "And the angel of the LORD found her by a fountain of water in the wilderness, by the fountain in the way to Shur" (**KJV**).

Later, when Hagar and Ishmael were sent away by Abraham and Sarah, the Bible says that an angel ministered unto them:

Genesis 21:17 - "And God heard the voice of the lad; and the angel of God called to Hagar out of heaven, and said unto her, 'What aileth thee, Hagar? fear not; for God hath heard the voice of the lad where he is'" **(KJV)**.

- ***Three Angels Visit Abraham***

The Bible says that three angels visited Abraham while on their way to Sodom. These angels appeared in the form of men.

Genesis 18:2 - "And he lift up his eyes and looked, and, lo, three men stood by him: and when he saw them, he ran to meet them from the tent door, and bowed himself toward the ground" **(KJV)**.

- ***Rescue Of Lot***

Two angels rescued Lot from the destruction of Sodom.

Genesis 19:16 - "And while he lingered, the men laid hold upon his hand, and upon the hand of his wife, and upon the hand of his two daughters; the LORD being merciful unto him: and they brought him forth, and set him without the city" **(KJV)**.

- ***Jacob***

Jacob had a variety of experiences with angels. One of these episodes was his famous dream.

Genesis 28:12 - "And he dreamed, and behold a ladder set up on the earth, and the top of it reached to heaven: and behold the angels of God ascending and descending on it" **(KJV)**.

> **Genesis 31:11** - "The angel of God spake unto me in a dream, saying, 'Jacob': And I said, Here am I'" **(KJV)**.

Later, angels met Jacob as he traveled.

> **Genesis 32:1** - "And Jacob went on his way, and the angels of God met him" **(KJV)**.

At the end of his life, Jacob said:

> **Genesis 48:16** - "The Angel which redeemed me from all evil, bless the lads; and let my name be named on them, and the name of my father Abraham and Isaac; and let them grow into a multitude in the midst of the earth" **(KJV)**.

- *Moses*

An angel of the Lord appeared to Moses to lead the Israelites from captivity in Egypt to the Promised Land.

> **Exodus 3:2** - "The angel of the LORD appeared to him in a blazing fire from the midst of a bush; and he looked, and behold, the bush was burning with fire, yet the bush was not consumed" **(NASB)**.

- *Passover Angel*

The angel of death killed every firstborn, of both humans and animals, of those families who did not have blood placed over their door post. The families of those who placed the blood were passed over:

> **Exodus 12:13** - "And the blood shall be to you for a token upon the houses where ye are: and when I see

the blood, I will pass over you, and the plague shall not be upon you to destroy you, when I smite the land of Egypt" (**KJV**).

- *Exodus*

God sends an angel to lead Moses.

Exodus 23:20-22 - "Behold, I am going to send an angel before you to guard you along the way and to bring you into the place which I have prepared. Be on your guard before him and obey his voice; do not be rebellious toward him, for he will not pardon your transgression, since My name is in him. But if you truly obey his voice and do all that I say, then I will be an enemy to your enemies and an adversary to your adversaries" (**NASB**).

- *Warning to Balaam*

God sent His angel to warn Balaam that he was disobeying the Lord.

Numbers 22:30-31 - "The donkey said to Balaam, 'Am I not your donkey on which you have ridden all your life to this day? Have I ever been accustomed to do so to you?' And he said, 'No.' Then the LORD opened the eyes of Balaam, and he saw the angel of the LORD standing in the way with his drawn sword in his hand; and he bowed all the way to the ground" (**NASB**).

- *Giving of Law*

Angels were present at the giving of the law.

Deuteronomy 33:2 - "He said, 'The LORD came from Sinai, And dawned on them from Seir; He shone forth from Mount Paran, And He came from the midst of ten thousand holy ones; At His right hand there was flashing lightning for them'" (**ASB**).

Psalm 68:17 - "The chariots of God are twenty thousand, even thousands of angels: the Lord is among them, as in Sinai, in the holy place" (**KJV**).

- *Rebuke of Israel*

An angel rebuked Israel for their idolatry.

Judges 2:1-4 - "And an angel of the LORD came up from Gilgal to Bochim, and said, I made you to go up out of Egypt, and have brought you unto the land which I sware unto your fathers; and I said, I will never break my covenant with you. And ye shall make no league with the inhabitants of this land; ye shall throw down their altars: but ye have not obeyed my voice: why have ye done this? Wherefore I also said, I will not drive them out from before you; but they shall be as thorns in your sides, and their gods shall be a snare unto you. And it came to pass, when the angel of the LORD spake these words unto all the children of Israel, that the people lifted up their voice, and wept" (**KJV**).

- *David*

God sent an angel to punish King David and the Israelites, but stopped the angel from destroying Jerusalem after King David repented and offered sacrifice to the Lord.

II Samuel 24:17 - "And David spake unto the LORD when he saw the angel that smote the people, and said, Lo, I have sinned, and I have done wickedly: but these sheep, what have they done? let thine hand, I pray thee, be against me, and against my father's house" **(KJV)**.

- *Curse Enemies Of The Lord*

Judges 5:23 - "Curse ye Meroz, said the angel of the LORD, curse ye bitterly the inhabitants thereof; because they came not to the help of the LORD, to the help of the LORD against the mighty" **(KJV)**.

- *Elijah*

When Elijah fled Jezebel after his triumph on Mount Carmel, an angel brought him food, giving him strength to meet the Lord on Mount Horeb in I Kings:

I Kings 19:5 - "And as he lay and slept under a juniper tree, behold, then an angel touched him, and said unto him, Arise and eat" **(KJV)**.

- *The Assyrians*

The angel of the LORD killed a large number of the Assyrian army.

II Kings 19:35 - "And it came to pass that night, that the angel of the LORD went out, and smote in the camp of the Assyrians an hundred fourscore and five thousand: and when they arose early in the morning, behold, they were all dead corpses" **(KJV)**.

- *Daniel*

Michael, as one of the leading angels, is considered "Prince" of the heavenly hosts, and appears several times in the Book of Daniel:

Daniel 6:19-22 - "Then the king arose very early in the morning, and went in haste unto the den of lions. And when he came to the den, he cried with a lamentable voice unto Daniel: and the king spake and said to Daniel, O Daniel, servant of the living God, is thy God, whom thou servest continually, able to deliver thee from the lions? Then said Daniel unto the king, O king, live for ever. My God hath sent his angel, and hath shut the lions' mouths, that they have not hurt me: forasmuch as before him innocency was found in me; and also before thee, O king, have I done no hurt" **(KJV)**.

Daniel 8:16 - "And I heard a man's voice between the banks of Ulai, which called, and said, Gabriel, make this man to understand the vision" **(KJV)**.

Daniel 9:21 - "Yea, whiles I was speaking in prayer, even the man Gabriel, whom I had seen in the vision at the beginning, being caused to fly swiftly, touched me about the time of the evening oblation" **(KJV)**.

Daniel 10:13 - "But the prince of the kingdom of Persia withstood me one and twenty days: but, lo, Michael, one of the chief princes, came to help me; and I remained there with the kings of Persia" **(KJV)**.

Daniel 10:21 - "But I will shew thee that which is noted in the scripture of truth: and there is none that holdeth with me in these things, but Michael your prince" **(KJV)**.

Daniel 12:1 - "And at that time shall Michael stand up, the great prince which standeth for the children of thy people: and there shall be a time of trouble, such as never was since there was a nation even to that same time: and at that time thy people shall be delivered, every one that shall be found written in the book" **(KJV)**.

- *Psalms*

Psalm 91:11-12 - "For He will give His angels charge concerning you, To guard you in all you ways. They will bear you up in their hands, That you do not strike your foot against a stone" **(KJV)**.

NEW TESTAMENT

- *Joseph*

An angel of the Lord appeared to Joseph three times in a dream first to make Mary his wife, to take the trip to Egypt, and then to return to Nazareth.

Matthew 1:18 -20 - "Now the birth of Jesus Christ was on this wise: When as his mother Mary was espoused to Joseph, before they came together, she was found with child of the Holy Ghost. Then Joseph her husband, being a just man, and not willing to make her a public example, was minded to put her away privily. But while he thought on these things, behold, the angel of the LORD appeared unto him in a dream, saying, Joseph, thou son of David, fear not to take unto thee Mary thy wife: for that which is conceived in her is of the Holy Ghost" **(KJV)**.

- *Mary*

Luke 1:26-28 - "And in the sixth month the angel Gabriel was sent from God unto a city of Galilee, named Nazareth, To a virgin espoused to a man whose name was Joseph, of the house of David; and the virgin's name was Mary. And the angel came in unto her, and said, Hail, thou that art highly favoured, the Lord is with thee: blessed art thou among women" **(KJV)**.

- *Shepherds*

Luke 2:14 - "Glory to God in the highest, and on earth peace among men with whom He is pleased" (**NASB**).

- *Christ in the Desert*

Angels minister to Christ.

Matthew 4:11 - "Then the devil left Him; and behold, angels came and *began* to minister to Him" (**NIV**).

- *Christ in the Garden*

Luke 22:43 - "Now an angel from heaven appeared to Him, strengthening Him" (**NIV**).

- *Resurrection*

John 20:12 - "And she saw two angels in white sitting, one at the head and one at the feet, where the body of Jesus had been lying" (**NIV**).

- *Stephen's Speech*

Acts 7:35 - "This Moses whom they disowned, saying, 'WHO MADE YOU A RULER AND A JUDGE?' is the one whom God sent *to be* both a ruler and a deliverer with the help of the angel who appeared to him in the thorn bush" (**NASB**).

Acts 7:38 - "This is the one who was in the congregation in the wilderness together with the angel who was speaking to him on Mount Sinai, and *who was* with our fathers; and he received living oracles to pass on to you" (**NASB**).

Acts 7:53 - "You who received the law as ordained by angels, and *yet* did not keep it" **(NASB)**.

- *Peter*

An angel rescues Peter from jail.

Acts 12:6-10 - "On the very night when Herod was about to bring him forward, Peter was sleeping between two soldiers, bound with two chains, and guards in front of the door were watching over the prison. And behold, an angel of the Lord suddenly appeared and a light shone in the cell; and he struck Peter's side and woke him up, saying, 'Get up quickly.' And his chains fell off his hands. And the angel said to him, 'Gird yourself and put on your sandals.' And he did so. And he said to him, 'Wrap your cloak around you and follow me.' And he went out and continued to follow, and he did not know that what was being done by the angel was real, but thought he was seeing a vision. When they had passed the first and second guard, they came to the iron gate that leads into the city, which opened for them by itself; and they went out and went along one street, and immediately the angel departed from him" **(NASB)**.

FUTURE EVENTS

Mark 13:32 - "But of that day or hour no one knows, not even the angels in heaven, nor the Son, but the Father alone" **(NASB)**.

Matthew 13:49 - "So it will be at the end of the age; the angels will come forth and take out the wicked from among the righteous" **(NIV)**.

Matthew 18:10 - "See that you do not despise one of these little ones, for I say to you that their angels in heaven continually see the face of My Father who is in heaven" **(NIV)**.

Matthew 24:31 - "And He will send forth His angels with A GREAT TRUMPET and THEY WILL GATHER TOGETHER His elect from the four winds, from one end of the sky to the other" **(NASB)**.

ANGELIC GATHERING

So you've never seen or heard an angel? Be patient, it will happen in time. As stated throughout this book there are numerous accounts of angels visiting the earth for specific purposes. The largest gathering of angels occurred when Jesus was born in a manger in the small town of Bethlehem. This is rather a lengthy passage of scripture but it gives details of the announcement of the birth of our Savior, Jesus Christ, the Son of God.

> **Luke 2:8-20** - "And there were in the same country shepherds abiding in the field, keeping watch over their flock by night. And, lo, the angel of the Lord came upon them, and the glory of the Lord shone round about them: and they were sore afraid. And the angel said unto them, Fear not: for, behold, I bring you good tidings of great joy, which shall be to all people. For unto you is born this day in the city of David a Saviour, which is Christ the Lord. And this shall be a sign unto you; Ye shall find the babe wrapped in swaddling clothes, lying in a manger. And suddenly there was with the angel a multitude of the heavenly host praising God, and saying, Glory to God in the highest, and on earth peace, good will toward men.

And it came to pass, as the angels were gone away from them into heaven, the shepherds said one to another, let us now go even unto Bethlehem, and see this thing which is come to pass, which the Lord hath made known unto us. And they came with haste, and found Mary, and Joseph, and the babe lying in a manger. And when they had seen it, they made known abroad the saying which was told them concerning this child. And all they that heard it wondered at those things which were told them by the shepherds. But Mary kept all these things, and pondered them in her heart. And the shepherds returned, glorifying and praising God for all the things that they had heard and seen, as it was told unto them" **(KJV)**.

Verse 13 in the paragraph above, reads: "And suddenly there was with the angel a multitude of the heavenly host praising God, ….". A multitude of angels were present on earth for one reason only and that was to see the birth of Christ. We are told a myriad of angels will once again descend to see the next big heavenly event on earth, a "Spectacle of a Lifetime."

Like John, we'll all someday see and hear "the voice of many angels, numbering thousands upon thousands, and ten thousand times ten thousand." With them we will praise the Savior singing, "Worthy is the Lamb, who was slain, to receive power and wealth and wisdom and strength and honor and glory and praise!" (Gangel, 1990).

Revelation 5:11-12 - "Then I looked, and I heard the voice of many angels surrounding the throne and the living creatures and the elders; they numbered myriads of myriads and thousands of thousands singing with full voice, "Worthy is the Lamb that was slaughtered to receive power and wealth and wisdom and might and honor and glory and blessing" **(RSV)**!

It is written that the return of Jesus to earth is said to be "on the clouds of the sky" and will be accompanied with awesome power and great glory. And He will send forth His angels with a great trumpet and they will gather together His elect from the four winds, from one end of the sky to the other:

> **Matthew 24:31** - "And he will send his angels with a loud trumpet call, and they will gather his elect from the four winds, from one end of the heavens to the other" **(NIV)**.

The whole premise of my writing this book is I believe angels are real creations of God and will come in intervals of time prior to the 2nd coming of the Lord. They are coming to view the place (earth) and the greatest event in Bible prophesy as well as the greatest event in human history:

THE COMING OF THE LORD JESUS CHRIST!

As already stated, angels are curious creatures and they will want to see where this **AWESOME EVENT** will take place. I believe a host of people will see, hear, and discern many encounters with **ANGELS** when they visit **EARTH** prior to this event coming to pass. The early followers of Jesus Christ knew He had ascended to heaven and they expected that He would return for them as promised.

Be spiritually prepared and watchful for His victorious return!

I Thessalonians 4:16-17 - "For the Lord himself shall descend from heaven with a shout, with the voice of the archangel, and with the trump

of God: and the dead in Christ shall rise first: Then we which are alive and remain shall be caught up together with them in the clouds, to meet the Lord in the air: and so shall we ever be with the Lord" (KJV).

Gathering of the Angels

Angels Walk Among Us

References

Blanchard, John, *Demons Servants of Satan*, Tabletalk Magazine, July 1, 2007.

Bushnell, James Oliver Jr., *A Systematic Theology of the Christian Religion*, Vol. 1, Zondervan, Grand Rapids, 1962.

Chafer, Lewis Sperry, *Systematic Theology*, Vol. 2, Kregel Publications, 1993.

Dickason, Fred C, *Names of Angels*, Moody Publishers, 1997.

Editors of Guideposts, *Angels In Our Midst*. Doubleday, New York, 1993.

Encyclopedia of the Unusual and Unexplained, *Guardian Angels*, Gale Research Inc. 2003.

Evans, William, *The Great Doctrines of the Bible*, Moody Press, Chicago, 1912.

Fry, Gill, *Encounters with Angels*, Share International, August 1999.

Gangel, Kenneth O, *Angels: An Endangered Species*, Simon & Schuster, 1990.

Godwin, Malcolm, *Angels: An Endangered Species*, Simon & Schuster, 1990.

Got Questions Ministries, *Who or what is Abaddon/Apollyon?*, February 15, 2017.

Graham, Dr. Billy, *Angels: God's Secret Agents*, Doubleday & Company Inc., 1975.

Jackson, Wayne, *The Growing Interest in Angels*, Christian Courier.com, February 4, 2019.

Metzger, Bruce M, *An Introduction to the Apocrypha*, New York: Oxford University Press, 1977.

Mueller, Chris, *Guardian Angels, Watch over Us*, Ascension Press, 2015.

Oehler, Gustav F. *Theology of the Old Testament*, Funk & Wagnalls, 1983.

Outlaw, Greg, *Angels and Demons*, AllAboutSpirituality.org, 2019.

Outlaw, Greg, *Fallen Angels*, AllAboutSpirituality.org, 2015.

Outlaw, Greg. *Guardian Angels*, AllAboutSpirituality.org, 2016.

Parente, Pascal P, *The Angels*. Published by TAN Books, December 3, 1994.

Ryrie, Charles C, *Basic Theology*, Victor Books, Wheaton, IL, 1987.

Slick, Matt, *What are the names of the angels in the Bible?*, Christian Apologetics and Research Ministry, Nampa, ID, 2013.

The Holy Bible, *English Standard Version Bible*, (ESV), New York: Oxford University Press, 2009.

The Holy Bible, *King James Version*, (KJV), New York: American Bible Society, 1999.

The Holy Bible, *New American Standard Bible*, (NASB), La Habra, CA: Foundation Publications, for the Lockman Foundation, 1971.

The Holy Bible, *New International Version*, (NIV), Grand Rapids: Zondervan Publishing House, 1984.

The Holy Bible, *New Living Translation*, (NLT), Tyndale House Foundation, 2015.

The Holy Bible, *New Revised Standard Version Bible*, (NRSV), Division of Christian Education of the National Council of the Churches of Christ in the United States of America, 1989.

Towns, Elmer L, *The Essence of the New Testament: A Survey*, B&H Publishing Group, 2016.

Wallace, Warner J, *Cold-Case Christianity*, David C Cook, 2013.

White, Lesli, *The Important Differences between Angels and Demons*, Publisher: David C. Cook, 2013.

APPENDIX
Angels – 100 Verses

Angels – 100 verses – ESV

Psalm 91:11

"For he will command his angels concerning you to guard you in all your ways."

Hebrews 3:2

"Do not neglect to show hospitality to strangers, for thereby some have entertained angels unawares."

Hebrews 13:2

"Do not neglect to show hospitality to strangers, for thereby some have entertained angels unawares."

Hebrews 1:14

"Are they not all ministering spirits sent out to serve for the sake of those who are to inherit salvation?"

Psalm 103:20

"Bless the Lord, O you his angels, you mighty ones who do his word, obeying the voice of his word!"

Psalm 34:7

"The angel of the Lord encamps around those who fear him, and delivers them."

Isaiah 6:2

"Above him stood the seraphim. Each had six wings: with two he covered his face, and with two he covered his feet, and with two he flew."

Jude 6

"And the angels who did not stay within their own position of authority, but left their proper dwelling, he has kept in eternal chains under gloomy darkness until the judgment of the great day."

Revelation 19:10

"Then I fell down at his feet to worship him, but he said to me, "You must not do that! I am a fellow servant with you and your brothers who hold to the testimony of Jesus. Worship God." For the testimony of Jesus is the spirit of prophecy."

Matthew 24:31

"And he will send out his angels with a loud trumpet call, and they will gather his elect from the four winds, from one end of heaven to the other."

Jude 9

"But when the archangel Michael, contending with the devil, was disputing about the body of Moses, he did not presume to pronounce a blasphemous judgment, but said, 'The Lord rebuke you.'"

Acts 27:23

"For this very night there stood before me an angel of the God to whom I belong and whom I worship."

Matthew 18;10

"See that you do not despise one of these little ones. For I tell you that in heaven their angels always see the face of my Father who is in heaven."

Acts 8:26

"Now an angel of the Lord said to Philip, 'Rise and go toward the south to the road that goes down from Jerusalem to Gaza.' This is a desert place."

Luke 15:10

"Just so, I tell you, there is joy before the angels of God over one sinner who repents."

Colossians 1:16

"For by him all things were created, in heaven and on earth, visible and invisible, whether thrones or dominions or rulers or authorities; all things were created through him and for him."

Judges 13:6

"Then the woman came and told her husband, "A man of God came to me, and his appearance was like the appearance of the angel of God, very awesome. I did not ask him where he was from, and he did not tell me his name."

Exodus 23:20

"Behold, I send an angel before you to guard you on the way and to bring you to the place that I have prepared."

Psalm 68:17

"The chariots of God are twice ten thousand, thousands upon thousands; the Lord is among them; Sinai is now in the sanctuary."

Revelation 22:6

"And he said to me, "These words are trustworthy and true. And the Lord, the God of the spirits of the prophets, has sent his angel to show his servants what must soon take place."

Acts 5:19

"But during the night an angel of the Lord opened the prison doors and brought them out, and said."

Mark 8:38

"For whoever is ashamed of me and of my words in this adulterous and sinful generation, of him will the Son of Man also be ashamed when he comes in the glory of his Father with the holy angels."

Matthew 13:41

"The Son of Man will send his angels, and they will gather out of his kingdom all causes of sin and all law-breakers."

Daniel 6:22

"My God sent his angel and shut the lions' mouths, and they have not harmed me, because I was found blameless before him; and also before you, O king, I have done no harm."

Matthew 24:36

"But concerning that day and hour no one knows, not even the angels of heaven, nor the Son, but the Father only."

Matthew 22:30

"For in the resurrection they neither marry nor are given in marriage, but are like angels in heaven."

Matthew 25:31

"When the Son of Man comes in his glory, and all the angels with him, then he will sit on his glorious throne."

Matthew 4:11

"Then the devil left him, and behold, angels came and were ministering to him."

II Kings 6:7

"Then Elisha prayed and said, "O Lord, please open his eyes that he may see." So the Lord opened the eyes of the young man, and he saw, and behold, the mountain was full of horses and chariots of fire all around Elisha."

Matthew 26:53

"Do you think that I cannot appeal to my Father, and he will at once send me more than twelve legions of angels?"

I Peter 1:12

"It was revealed to them that they were serving not themselves but you, in the things that have now been announced to you through those who preached the good news to you by the Holy Spirit sent from heaven, things into which angels long to look."

Matthew 1:20

"But as he considered these things, behold, an angel of the Lord appeared to him in a dream, saying, "Joseph, son of David, do not fear to take Mary as your wife, for that which is conceived in her is from the Holy Spirit."

I Timothy 5:21

"In the presence of God and of Christ Jesus and of the elect angels I charge you to keep these rules without prejudging, doing nothing from partiality."

Acts 7:3

"You who received the law as delivered by angels and did not keep it."

Acts 12:23

"Immediately an angel of the Lord struck him down, because he did not give God the glory, and he was eaten by worms and breathed his last."

Revelation 10:1-6

"Then I saw another mighty angel coming down from heaven, wrapped in a cloud, with a rainbow over his head, and his face was like the sun, and his legs like pillars of fire. He had a little scroll open in his hand. And he set his right foot on the sea, and his left foot on the land, and called out with a loud voice, like a lion roaring. When he called out, the seven thunders sounded. And when the seven thunders had sounded, I was about to write, but I heard a voice from heaven saying, "Seal up what the seven thunders have said, and do not write it down." And the angel whom I saw standing on the sea and on the land raised his right hand to heaven and swore by him who lives forever and ever, who created heaven and what is in it, the earth and what is in it, and the sea and what is in it, that there would be no more delay."

Luke 16:22

"The poor man died and was carried by the angels to Abraham's side. The rich man also died and was buried."

Psalm 148:2

"Praise him, all his angels; praise him, all his hosts!"

Hebrews 1:7

"Of the angels he says, 'He makes his angels winds, and his ministers a flame of fire.'"

Matthew 2:13

"Now when they had departed, behold, an angel of the Lord appeared to Joseph in a dream and said, "Rise, take the child and his mother, and flee to Egypt, and remain there until I tell you, for Herod is about to search for the child, to destroy him."

Luke 4:10

"For it is written, 'He will command his angels concerning you, to guard you.'"

II Chronicles 3:7-14

"So he lined the house with gold—its beams, its thresholds, its walls, and its doors—and he carved cherubim on the walls. And he made the Most Holy Place. Its length, corresponding to the breadth of the house, was twenty cubits, and its breadth was twenty cubits. He overlaid it with 600 talents of fine gold. The weight of gold for the nails was fifty shekels. And he overlaid the upper chambers with gold. In the Most Holy Place he made two cherubim of wood and overlaid them with gold. The wings of the cherubim together extended twenty cubits: one wing of the one, of five cubits, touched the wall of the house, and its other wing, of five cubits, touched the wing of the other cherub; ...".

Revelation 12:7

"Now war arose in heaven, Michael and his angels fighting against the dragon. And the dragon and his angels fought back."

Matthew 2:29

"But when Herod died, behold, an angel of the Lord appeared in a dream to Joseph in Egypt."

Psalm 103:21

"Bless the Lord, all his hosts, his ministers, who do his will!"

Psalm 8:5

"Yet you have made him a little lower than the heavenly beings and crowned him with glory and honor."

II Kings 19:35

"And that night the angel of the Lord went out and struck down 185,000 in the camp of the Assyrians. And when people arose early in the morning, behold, these were all dead bodies."

Exodus 14:19

"Then the angel of God who was going before the host of Israel moved and went behind them, and the pillar of cloud moved from before them and stood behind them."

Genesis 16:7

"The angel of the Lord found her by a spring of water in the wilderness, the spring on the way to Shur."

Revelation 22:9

"But he said to me, "You must not do that! I am a fellow servant with you and your brothers the prophets, and with those who keep the words of this book. Worship God."

Revelation 1:1

"The revelation of Jesus Christ, which God gave him to show to his servants the things that must soon take place. He made it known by sending his angel to his servant John."

I Thessalonians 4:16

"For the Lord himself will descend from heaven with a cry of command, with the voice of an archangel, and with the sound of the trumpet of God. And the dead in Christ will rise first."

John 1:51

"And he said to him, "Truly, truly, I say to you, you will see heaven opened, and the angels of God ascending and descending on the Son of Man."

Daniel 9:21

"While I was speaking in prayer, the man Gabriel, whom I had seen in the vision at the first, came to me in swift flight at the time of the evening sacrifice."

Isaiah 63:9

"In all their affliction he was afflicted, and the angel of his presence saved them; in his love and in his pity he redeemed them; he lifted them up and carried them all the days of old."

I Chronicles 21:15

"And God sent the angel to Jerusalem to destroy it, but as he was about to destroy it, the Lord saw, and he relented from the calamity. And he said to the angel who was working destruction, 'It is enough; now stay your hand.' And the angel of the Lord was standing by the threshing floor of Ornan the Jebusite."

Numbers 22:35

"And the angel of the Lord said to Balaam, 'Go with the men, but speak only the word that I tell you.' So Balaam went on with the princes of Balak."

Revelation 22:8

"I, John, am the one who heard and saw these things. And when I heard and saw them, I fell down to worship at the feet of the angel who showed them to me."

Hebrews 12:22

"But you have come to Mount Zion and to the city of the living God, the heavenly Jerusalem, and to innumerable angels in festal gathering."

Colossians 2:18

"Let no one disqualify you, insisting on asceticism and worship of angels, going on in detail about visions, puffed up without reason by his sensuous mind."

Ephesians 3:10

"So that through the church the manifold wisdom of God might now be made known to the rulers and authorities in the heavenly places."

John 20:12

"And she saw two angels in white, sitting where the body of Jesus had lain, one at the head and one at the feet."

Luke 20:36

"For they cannot die anymore, because they are equal to angels and are sons of God, being sons of the resurrection."

Luke 2:13

"And suddenly there was with the angel a multitude of the heavenly host praising God and saying."

Matthew 28:3

"His appearance was like lightning, and his clothing white as snow."

Matthew 13:49

"So it will be at the close of the age. The angels will come out and separate the evil from the righteous."

Psalm 35:5

"Let them be like chaff before the wind, with the angel of the Lord driving them away!"

Nehemiah 9:6

"You are the Lord, you alone. You have made heaven, the heaven of heavens, with all their host, the earth and all that is on it, the seas and all that is in them; and you preserve all of them; and the host of heaven worships you."

Genesis 3:24

"He drove out the man, and at the east of the garden of Eden he placed the cherubim and a flaming sword that turned every way to guard the way to the tree of life."

Hebrews 2:2

"For since the message declared by angels proved to be reliable, and every transgression or disobedience received a just retribution."

II Thessalonians 1:7

"And to grant relief to you who are afflicted as well as to us, when the Lord Jesus is revealed from heaven with his mighty angels."

Acts 1:11

"And said, "Men of Galilee, why do you stand looking into heaven? This Jesus, who was taken up from you into heaven, will come in the same way as you saw him go into heaven."

Luke 1:11-20

"And there appeared to him an angel of the Lord standing on the right side of the altar of incense. And Zechariah was troubled when he saw him, and fear fell upon him. But the angel said to him, "Do not be afraid, Zechariah, for your prayer has been heard, and your wife Elizabeth will bear you a son, and you shall call his name John. And you will have joy and gladness, and many will rejoice at his birth, for he will be great before the Lord. And he must not drink wine or strong drink, and he will be filled with the Holy Spirit, even from his mother's womb …"".

Mark 13:27

"And then he will send out the angels and gather his elect from the four winds, from the ends of the earth to the ends of heaven."

Mark 1:13

"And he was in the wilderness forty days, being tempted by Satan. And he was with the wild animals, and the angels were ministering to him."

Job 38:7

"When the morning stars sang together and all the sons of God shouted for joy?"

II Samuel 24:16

"And when the angel stretched out his hand toward Jerusalem to destroy it, the Lord relented from the calamity and said to the angel who was working destruction among the people, 'It is enough; now stay your hand.' And the angel of the Lord was by the threshing floor of Araunah the Jebusite."

Genesis 2:1

"Thus the heavens and the earth were finished, and all the host of them."

Hebrews 1:6

"And again, when he brings the firstborn into the world, he says, "Let all God's angels worship him."

Luke 9:31

"Who appeared in glory and spoke of his departure, which he was about to accomplish at Jerusalem."

Luke 4:11

"And 'On their hands they will bear you up, lest you strike your foot against a stone.'"

Luke 1:26-38

"In the sixth month the angel Gabriel was sent from God to a city of Galilee named Nazareth, to a virgin betrothed to a man whose name was Joseph, of the house of David. And the virgin's name was Mary. And he came to her and said, "Greetings, O favored one, the Lord is with you!" But she was greatly troubled at the saying, and tried to discern what sort of greeting this might be. And the angel said to her, "Do not be afraid, Mary, for you have found favor with God. ...".

Zechariah 5:9

"Then I lifted my eyes and saw, and behold, two women coming forward! The wind was in their wings. They had wings like the wings of a stork, and they lifted up the basket between earth and heaven."

Psalm 104:4

"He makes his messengers winds, his ministers a flaming fire."

I Kings 19:5

"And he lay down and slept under a broom tree. And behold, an angel touched him and said to him, 'Arise and eat.'"

II Samuel 14:17

"And your servant thought, 'The word of my lord the king will set me at rest,' for my lord the king is like the angel of God to discern good and evil. The Lord your God be with you!"

Jude 1:14

"It was also about these that Enoch, the seventh from Adam, prophesied, saying, "Behold, the Lord comes with ten thousands of his holy ones."

I Peter 3:22

"Who has gone into heaven and is at the right hand of God, with angels, authorities, and powers having been subjected to him."

Ezekiel 28:14-16

"You were an anointed guardian cherub. I placed you; you were on the holy mountain of God; in the midst of the stones of fire you walked. You were blameless in your ways from the day you were created, till unrighteousness was found in you. In the abundance of your trade you were filled with violence in your midst, and you sinned; so I cast you as a profane thing from the mountain of God, and I destroyed you, O guardian cherub, from the midst of the stones of fire."

Psalm 35:6

"Let their way be dark and slippery, with the angel of the Lord pursuing them!"

Hebrews 1:13

"And to which of the angels has he ever said, 'Sit at my right hand until I make your enemies a footstool for your feet?'"

Luke 9:30

"And behold, two men were talking with him, Moses and Elijah."

II Kings 1:15

"Then the angel of the Lord said to Elijah, "Go down with him; do not be afraid of him." So he arose and went down with him to the king."

II Samuel 19:27

"He has slandered your servant to my lord the king. But my lord the king is like the angel of God; do therefore what seems good to you."

II Samuel 14:20

"In order to change the course of things your servant Joab did this. But my lord has wisdom like the wisdom of the angel of God to know all things that are on the earth."

Luke 20:35

"But those who are considered worthy to attain to that age and to the resurrection from the dead neither marry nor are given in marriage."

Matthew 4:6

"And said to him, 'If you are the Son of God, throw yourself down, for it is written, He will command his angels concerning you,' and 'On their hands they will bear you up, lest you strike your foot against a stone.'"

Ezekiel 10:12-14

"And their whole body, their rims, and their spokes, their wings, and the wheels were full of eyes all around—the wheels that the four of them had. As for the wheels, they were called in my hearing "the whirling wheels." And every one had four faces: the first face was the face of the cherub, and the second face was a human face, and the third the face of a lion, and the fourth the face of an eagle."

Luke 15:7

"Just so, I tell you, there will be more joy in heaven over one sinner who repents than over ninety-nine righteous persons who need no repentance."

Daniel 7:10

"A stream of fire issued and came out from before him; a thousand thousands served him, and ten thousand times ten thousand stood before him; the court sat in judgment, and the books were opened."

Matthew 17:3

"And behold, there appeared to them Moses and Elijah, talking with him."

Photos of Angels
by Don Litton

Angels Walk Among Us

Angel picture in the sanctuary of Friendship Baptist Church, Fishville, LA

Angel picture in the sanctuary of Faith Tabernacle Shreveport La

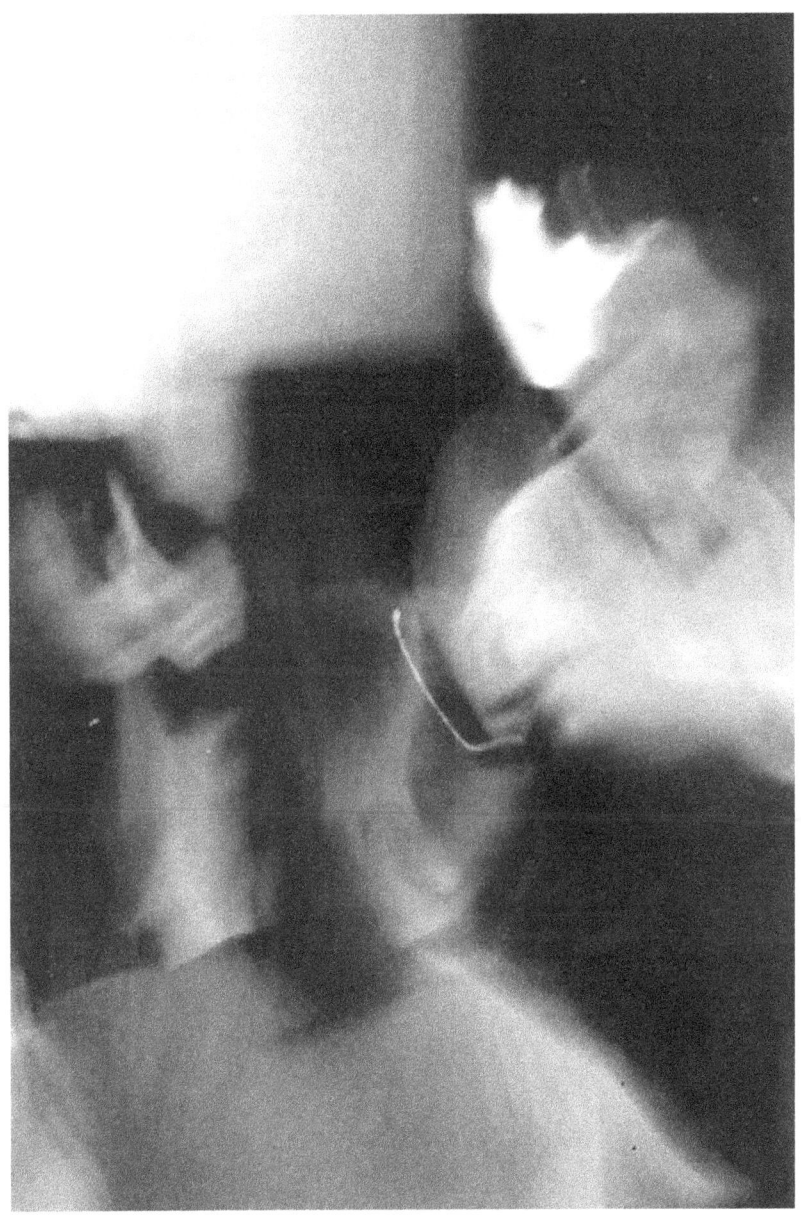

Pastor Don Litton praying for the sick when a hand of fire came on his head